ALLEN COUNTY PUBLIC LIBRARY

ACPL ITEM

DISCARDED

3 1833 06231

P9-BIO-291

FEB 24 '65

Tragedy in the Art of Music

The Charles Eliot Norton Lectures
1962 – 1963

Tragedy in the Art of Music

By LEO SCHRADE

HARVARD UNIVERSITY PRESS

Cambridge, Massachusetts

1 9 6 4

© Copyright 1964 by the President and Fellows of Harvard College
All rights reserved

Distributed in Great Britain by Oxford University Press, London

Library of Congress Catalog Card Number 64-10444

Printed in the United States of America

1287195

To Otto Kinkeldey,
Nestor of American musicology, in admiration

Preface

The first of my duties to be discharged—with unfeigned feeling rather than eloquence—is the most pleasant of all: the duty of rendering my thanks to all those who have taken it upon themselves to invite me to Harvard University.

The great honor which comes to the Charles Eliot Norton Professor of Poetry must not be measured in any other terms than those of obligation. And obligation to the Norton Chair accrues, indeed, from its illustrious tradition established by many a man of prodigious distinction. Fully conscious of the tradition I cannot say that my mind is at ease. Still less comfortable do I feel if I think that the tradition holds a further implication of burdensome renown, and one that does not seem to be commonly known. Hence I beg the favor of your attention for a brief story—and a story it is—with which to clarify what must appear as a baffling allusion.

In a letter dated July 3, 1870, Jacob Burckhardt wrote Friedrich von Preen that he was greatly surprised to see his friend occupied with the study of the *Cicerone*, a book which Burckhardt completed at the age of 37 in 1855; he said at the time when he wrote the *Cicerone*, a time free of care and caution as it becomes the age of a young author, he did not expect that the book would be taken as seriously as it had been by many an excellent person ever since its appearance; and then he continued: "Recently, an American came up to my room to develop *a whole theory* the *starting point of which* he took from a passage in the *Cicerone* concerning *the asymmetry of romanesque buildings.* I had considerable trouble in making him understand how remote from art and art literature I was at the time."

Who was the American visitor? Here we follow the story in accordance with the eminent Burckhardt scholar Werner Kaegi (*Europäische Horizonte im Denken Jacob Burckhardts,* Basel–Stuttgart, 1962, pp. 76f, 170f). It has been suggested that the visitor might have been Henry Adams, an early admirer of Burckhardt, who would seem to have reviewed the *Civilization of the Renaissance in Italy* in a brilliant article, "The Genesis of Modern Life," which appeared anonymously in the *New York Herald* of 1880. As a matter of fact, Henry Adams was in Europe and even in Switzerland in 1870, but not in Basel; and so the suggestion has been withdrawn.

At all events, the visitor must have been a man not only familiar with the *Cicerone,* but also at least to a degree an adherent of Burckhardt's ideas.

Now we read the following passage in the appendix to a famous book: "Few of the writers on the architecture of the Middle Ages refer to it," meaning the "irregularities of construction in Italian buildings of the Middle Ages." "Burckhardt, in his *Cicerone,*" so the author continues, "attributes *the irregularities* to 'an indifference to mathematical exactness peculiar to the early Middle Ages', which seems to exclude *the idea of a guiding aesthetic sentiment* and an exquisite aesthetic result." The book has the title *Historical Studies of Church-Building in the Middle Ages.* It appeared in 1880, and its author was Charles Eliot Norton.

And Charles Eliot Norton went to Switzerland, not in 1870, but in 1869. Among the Norton papers, held by the

Houghton Library, there are two letters, one written to James Russell Lowell dated June 14, 1869, the other to Henry Wadsworth Longfellow dated June 17, 1869, and in both Norton mentions that on his extended journey undertaken for the sake of art studies he came from England, passed through Antwerp and along the Rhine, and stopped at Basel before reaching Vevey and his prolonged stay in Italy. It was not the first time that he had visited Basel. When still a young student, 23 years of age, he had communicated to his family, in a letter dated September 26, 1850, his impressions of the city, and in particular the fascination the tombstone of Erasmus with its inscription had for him.

The most likely visitor whom Burckhardt referred to in his letter would appear to be Charles Eliot Norton; and an intriguing thought it is, indeed, if we imagine that through Burckhardt and Norton the University of Basel and this distinguished chair at Harvard University may well be linked together by a personal association which would be almost a century old.

Last but not least, I wish to express my sincerest thanks: to the President and Fellows of Harvard College to whom I owe the honor of having been appointed to the Norton lectures; to the members of the Department of Music who made the sojourn in Cambridge most enjoyable; to Professor Laurence Wylie, acting Master, and Mrs. Wylie for the hospitality of Quincy House; to Professor William Alexander Jackson and the staff at the Houghton Library for the assistance given to my wife and myself in our search among the Norton papers; and to Mr. Wulf Arlt, Basel, who prepared the index.

June 1963

Leo Schrade

Contents

Tragedy in the Art of Music

I

The Theme

Ancient representations of Melpomene, however late their appearance, are wont to depict the Muse adorned with a garland of vine leaves, both a club and a mask in her hands, the vine leaves being a tribute to Dionysus, the club belonging to Heracles, and the mask betokening the tragedy.

The raving god—Zeus-begotten, but borne by mortal Semele—Dionysus, who harbors the elements of life and death, himself now dead and lost to sight, now rising from the depths of the ocean, or from the unfathomable lake, Alkyonia, or from Hades, having rested there "in the house of Persephone," rising to vindicate his epiphany time and again like the cyclic rhythm of the seasons—he, the god of frenzy, is the god of tragedy. "All the world will soon be dancing when Bromios leads his roaming throngs to the mountain where the women flock together chased away from the weaving-loom and the shuttle by the thyrsus of Dionysus." Thus, *The Bacchae* of Euripides describes the effect of the god whenever he makes his striking appearance.

And Heracles, though man, at last, with the twelve labors and many another exploit heroically accomplished, transported from the pyre high on the mountain Oeta to the divine abode of gods immortal; beginner of human civilization and founder of sacred feasts; leader of the Muses, too,

Musagetes like Dionysus and Apollo; the hero who has been immortalized not only as a dweller in Olympus, but also by the poet's fancy in epic and drama—he is the ever present genius of dramatic art. Did he not snatch Alcestis from the grasp of Pluto? Did he not inspire the poet to celebrate his deeds time after time? His famous club, testimonial to his heroic work, becomes the symbol of his patronage of drama.

And the tragic Muse. Daughters of Zeus and Mnemosyne, the Muses, "the mindful ones," have been singing to the gods, according to Homer, ever since Zeus raised them to be goddesses in the Olympian dwelling. Although the musical faculty is their prime distinction, their endowments have a vast range. With Mnemosyne, Memory, being their mother, they know mankind from the days of yore; they have the vision to prophesy events of the future as they seem to have shared in dispensing the Delphian oracle. In olden times, there were but three Muses: Melete, the Muse of meditative practice and judicious skill; Mneme, the Muse of memory requisite for recording notable deeds to be recalled at all times to come; and Aoide, the Muse of song which allows the marvelous tales to ring out. Thus, music skillfully rendered by Melete, inspired by Mneme, speaks of the story of man, past, present, and future. Further still, the tragic Muse, the mask of tragedy, becomes the image of human passion and despair, "expressed"—to speak with the words of Henry James—"in the divinest, truest music that had ever poured from tragic lips."

With music of such divine truth Melpomene enchants men "even if their ears were plugged up with wax." Yet the divine truth cannot be but the truth of Dionysus. The god himself, as Pausanias reports, is named "Dionysus Melpomenos" as proverbially as Apollo is called Musagetes. Melpomene's song then resounds with "the tragic fury" of the god, and it abounds with the eloquence of which she is the lavish benefactress granting—as Hesiod bears witness—the flow of words to all who drank from the waters of the Helicon where the Muses possessed a temple of their own.

The music of the tragedy, Dionysus the tragic singer, the song of the tragic Muse—this is our first and foremost theme. It must be said that neither whim nor an ambitious twist of mind but clear necessity has taken us upon the highway to the Greek world of thought. For joined together in wedlock everlasting and inseparable, Greek music and Greek drama stand at the threshold of "Tragedy in the Art of Music." So close did the wondrous concord appear to be in fact that Greek tragedy was found to owe its birth to the spirit of music.

But the music of Greek tragedy also stands on the threshold of the conceptions that western man contrived to bring to the music of the drama. To be sure, late Hellenistic tragedy no longer may have shown the original unity of music and drama; it may at last have yielded to a divorce of the elements from the bonds of marriage, thus allowing each partner to take its own course; it certainly lost itself entirely in the obscurity of dark ages. But when the hour had come for the music drama to reappear, Greek tragedy stood at its side like a sponsor whose measure of responsibility matched his wealth of experience.

Despite such noble sponsorship, the tragic Muse was quick to change her ancient attribute, the mask; or perhaps the dramatists of recent arrival were bound to put a new-fangled mask upon the venerable face of old. The composers

of the new music drama took recourse to their Greek ances-
tors for the benefit of shaping thought and stimulating fancy,
even of setting the goal for every ambition and endeavor.
They were, however, charmed by all the resplendent properties, perhaps but mere accidents, of Greek tragedy, and
unknowingly, yet unavoidably, they failed to penetrate to
the substance. Not that the complete loss of Greek music,
the music which they thought to revive—if what they accomplished could ever have been a revival—had been the
main reason for their failure. Their restoration of Greek
tragedy, more imaginary than real, was debarred from ever
being complete because the Greek concept of tragedy had
been eclipsed largely by the intervention of Christian ideas,
and no humanistic effort could repair its authenticity.

However painstakingly the western dramatists obeyed
the precepts of drama—if precepts they were—in deference
to Aristotle's *Poetics*, they did not notice, or they did not
want to see, that the essence of Greek tragedy never rested
upon the famous laws. Indeed, Aristotle's laws seem to have
been singled out for an unduly magnified distinction because
there was no way of assenting to the essence without coming
to grips with the Christian doctrine of Providence. For the
essence of tragedy lay in the Greek concept of Fate bound
up with Greek religion and religious cults.

The music newly wedded to the drama may still speak
of human passion and despair, still be of the "divinest,
truest" kind, but it is now no longer "the tragic fury" of
the god Dionysus that sounds from behind the tragic mask.
In Greek tragedy we search after the Dionysian nature and
the extent to which its music was allowed to range; in the
new music drama our search pertains to the display and

extent of the tragic. With our theme thus being completely recast, the new music drama brings us face to face with altogether different considerations.

But do the tones of the tragedy always mean the same as tragic tones? In other words, is it that only the association of music and drama makes it possible to permeate tones with the tragic feeling? The musical expression of the tragic has asserted itself in many ways and many a time apart from the tragedy proper, even without any text as a partner. Whoever has not experienced tragic tones of music sharper and more piercing than any music of a tragedy? But here we tread on perilous grounds. Since all such experiences consist of subjective impressions, perhaps unproved and seemingly unprovable, we necessarily embark upon adventurous excursions into the province of probability; hence "light be the tread of the sandal."

No matter what the degree of probability bearing upon the intuitive perception of feelings such as that of the tragic expressed in music, feelings, emotions, are as undeniable realities of human life as any event or fact that impresses itself upon our mind. *He pathe, to pathos,* pathos—pain, suffering, misfortune, and also passion—is, in the Greek sense, always a physical or mental condition, hence as such a reality of human existence; and *pathos poiein,* to make, to render, the presentation of passion in written or oral form, is known, in Aristotle's *Rhetoric,* as an idiom of Greek rhetoricians. The expression of the tragic, surely the most intimate consort forever attendant to the presentation of passions, belongs to what can be called the rhetoric of music, although we must admit the rhetorical figures to have lost much of their obligatory quality in the music of more recent times, particularly during the nineteenth century. Nevertheless, the tragic character artistically shaped in music old and new cannot be but a part of our theme.

Not having reached as yet the end of our quick voyage through the realm of tragedy, we now must move on toward certain problems which, though different in kind, still come within the purview of our subject: one bears upon the properties of the historical situation, the other upon the temperament of the individual artist. Neither encloses the tragic as an element being always effective within the frame of its very nature; but both comprise it as a potential disposition. Not every situation or period of cultural history exhibits a constellation from which the tragic is to be inferred; nor does the tragic lie hidden in the nature of every artist, although the latter can scarcely be maintained with unconditional assurance.

Jacob Burckhardt once said: "Nicht jede Zeit findet ihren grossen Mann, und nicht jede grosse Fähigkeit findet ihre Zeit." (Not every epoch lights upon its great man, and not every great faculty falls in with its time.) Thus, committed to his environment and time, the artist appears on the scene under a constellation of circumstances which, whether favorable or unfavorable, affects the fortune of his work, that is, affects the historical position his work will be granted by his own time. With the fixed constellation being beyond his grasp and power there is something in the nature of fate that governs both his own self and the conditions into which he is born. Saying that a man was "born in the wrong time" is but an admission that his lot has been cast by an unfavorable fate.

The interaction of the two components, a given historical

situation and the great artist, may call forth a discord harsh enough to charge both the life and the work of the artist with the purport of tragedy. Apart from the dependence upon historical conditions, each bent that determines the inner life of the great man—the temperament, the natural disposition, the profundity of vision—may have all the makings of a tragic configuration. Hegel declared that in general the moral, tragic fate always would rest upon the conflict of two different rights, both of equal validity but opposed to each other, with the final result that one right would abolish the other; and on these grounds the fate of Socrates appeared to him as genuinely tragic. Be this as it may, neither the tragic nor tragedy seems ever to have come to pass without the interference of a superior, divine force, Fate, the ruler and true actor of the drama.

Tyche, Moira, Daimon, personified or abstract, single or combined, represent the divine force which has proved itself as the most powerful agent not only within the framework of Greek tragedy or of the drama, generally speaking, but also in the life of all great men.

Tyche, Fate, refers, in the first place, to that which *tynchanei*, to that which happens; all occurrences are, therefore, *tychai*, or in the words of Plato "nearly all human affairs are *tychai*." But all occurrences are made to come to pass; they are directed, dispatched, as it were, by Tyche, the goddess. Fate is that which is sent to man from above, the "portion" or lot which comes to every man at the hour of his birth. Thus, Tyche, and likewise Moira, are the distributors of the share man is to have in life. All things, gifts and endowments, have been given by Tyche and Moira. *Panta tyche kai moira andri dedoken*, so Archilochus says, and only by the mark of Fate does man rise above the common level. Great men owe their faculty of attaining to eminence to the intervention of Tyche with whom, according to Pindar, they seem to have a particularly intimate intercourse. Being the authors of history they are, in consequence of their distinction, more exposed than others to the perilous whims of Fate.

These exceptional men are keenly aware that Tyche in her speedy ways parcels out all the vicissitudes of life, the sudden changes and abrupt turns, the *metabolai, metastrophai, katastrophai*. Knowing the nature of Fate, they thoroughly distrust all operations of Tyche and Moira, and all the more are they put on the alert, even to extreme suspicion, if Fate should have granted her favors with all too generous abundance. As Herodotus writes in a letter: "I have not heard of anyone who did not tumble down disgracefully in the end if before he had had nothing but good fortune"; and, again according to Herodotus, Solon is reported to have said to Croesus—the chronological incongruity in the statement need be of no concern to us—that the gods have shown luck and prosperity to many men only to shatter them afterwards all the more thoroughly. When Philip of Macedonia received three happy messages in a row he stretched out his arms toward heaven praying that the Demon should add a moderate loss; for he was convinced that envy of too great a fortune appertained to the nature of Tyche. But it is Theognis who has drawn the most desperate conclusion from the merciless and blind actions of Fate. "Never to be born," he exclaims with the legendary words of Silenus, "never to have seen the light of the sun, this verily is the happiest lot of mankind; next best off is the man who after birth swiftly travels toward the gateway of Hades and rests deep down in his grave."

This calamitous judgment may appear to condemn life altogether for its futility; and yet, it is but the ultimate consequence of the belief, held without regret, self-pity, or sentimentality, that man is doomed by his inexorable fate to suffer in past, present, and future; and of this does the choir sing in Sophocles' *Antigone* as though it followed the example of the Moirai who, singing, announce the human destiny. But such a belief supplies the stuff that tragedy is made of, because it penetrates every action and appearance with the tragic potential.

Finally there is the Daimon, Demon, which stands at the side of Tyche and Moira as a divine being of Fate. The Demon joins the divinities which allot Fate to man, and with this capacity it is, god or goddess, among the distributors of human lots. Moira, Tyche, and Daimon often have so close a fellowship in their action that nothing short of sophistry will keep them apart as distinct entities. If the Daimon is called *Moiragetes*, the guide of fate, his function can hardly be differentiated from that of Moira herself.

It seems, however, that the Daimon has been associated predominantly with the fate of the individual. This accounts for the fact that he was looked upon as the tutelary genius of man. Perhaps in connection with the legend related by Hesiod that the demons were the human souls of the golden age which, after paradise was lost, lived midway between heaven and earth and watched over the deeds of men in order to protect them, the demons were thought to be the intermediaries between man and god.

Pindar imagined the demons as protective spirits which accompany man through life from the time of his birth; and for Plato, the demons were guardians. There is a fragment of Menander with verses saying that a demon joins each human being at the moment of his birth, a good demon who will lead each man through the whole of his life. Epictetus thought that it was Zeus who placed a guardian at the side of everybody, a demon who never sleeps and never lets himself be deceived. Hence we never should fancy that we are alone if we close the doors and darken our room, for we are not. God and our demon are with us; to see what we do, they need no light. As soldiers take an oath upon Caesar, we should swear upon this god, our demon.

The eternal enigma of the extraordinary man and his nature has been illustrated—for solved it never will be—by the intervention of the demon. The state of being possessed by the demon verifies distinction and greatness, and especially such a gift as we attribute to the creative artist. When Euripides in his *Bacchae* portrayed the boundless powers of the god Dionysus, he also praised the gift of prophetic vision. Named Daimon, the god, himself a prophet, accords his faculty to his devoted followers.

> A prophet is this God: the Bacchic frenzy
> And ecstasy are full-fraught with prophecy:
> For, in his fullness when he floods our frame,
> He makes his maddened votaries tell the future.

This vision, an endowment of those possessed by the god or the demon, belongs to the nature of the creative faculty. It is because of the visionary gift that the artist sees and knows more than the common man. As the Moirai, the goddesses of Fate, are said to be *bathyphrones*, deep-thinking, hence profound in their knowledge and vision, so the artist acquires extraordinary wisdom due to the communication with his demon. "Like the veil of things as they seem drawn back by an *unseen hand*. For a second you see—and seeing the secret, are the secret," says Edmund in O'Neill's *Long Day's Journey into Night*.

We still understand the word "demonic" to mean inspired by a superior force or a supernatural genius, guided by an unseen hand. Indeed, the *daimonios*, the demonic one, is the exceptional man whom nature singled out when departing from its regular course. Exceptional powers of thought, vision, and prescience have been infused into him who appears to grow to a godlike size, and for this he is viewed with awe as though he were a supernatural being. Plato spoke of such an exceptional man as the *sophos daimonios aner*. But those possessed by an evil demon, likewise unusual, distinct if not great, are the baleful ones, the wicked and the blind, and so they were addressed by Homer.

It lies in the nature of the demonic that man lives under a compulsory pressure if he lives in accordance with his demon for good or for evil. The celebrated *daimonion* of Socrates, described by Plato and more amply verified by Xenophon, appears to have implied but a limited effect of the demonic nature because, by manifesting itself as an "inner voice," the *daimonion* merely prevented Socrates from doing things if action was inopportune and the prospect of the outcome ill-starred. Never did the voice utter a positive command; nor, according to Plato, did the voice involve matters of great consequence.

A truly and fully demonic personality, however, implicates the whole human character, that is, whenever the Demon, "in his fullness," enters its being. Only then does man bear the full-blown impact of the divine force which drives him onward to fulfill his task whatever it may be. The demonic nature is a condition which determines his conduct as a whole. He attains his ends by discharging the duties to his demon; acting, as it were, always upon the command of his god, he expends his energies to the limit of his nature. But since, in the words of Epicharmos, "the character, *tropos,* is to many men the good demon, to others the evil one," these vehement energies may be spent for the good or for the bad. Atreus, the sinister tyrant in Seneca's tragedy *Thyestes,* surely the very incarnation of wickedness, holds the irresistible compulsion of his demon, an inner force that carries him away, to be responsible for all his dreadful deeds.

In any case, the close communion with the demon develops the fabric of the exceptional man. But it also imparts to all his actions and his manner of conduct a confidence beyond measure. All demonic men seem to have so cunning an assuredness of their proceeding and so little fear, if not complete unawareness, of any danger that they often strike the onlooker with paralyzing terror. Such being their fabric, the latent potential of the tragic which they possess as a natural disposition seems to surpass any other propensity to the condition of the tragic being.

Few men have given as much thought to the nature of the demonic as did Goethe and especially so late in his life when he occupied himself more intensely than ever with the mysterious nature of creative productivity and its relationship to the divine. The topic turns up in his autobiography, *Dichtung und Wahrheit,* and again many a time in his conversations with Eckermann. He admitted his ideas to be remarkably akin to the Greek conceptions, and, indeed, they are, though appearing in a new light and fraught with new significance. Greek thought penetrated his understanding of the demonic which determines every creative productivity. For he, too, believed that the demonic takes possession of the creative man, that it acts most powerfully as it pleases, that it subdues the possessed one into unconscious surrender, while the creative man still imagines that he acts of his own accord. "In such cases, man must often be regarded as the tool of a higher rulership, as the chosen vessel worthy of receiving the divine influence."

At times Goethe intermingled the demonic with the image of being possessed by a demon more evil than good, and this seems to be at the basis of his general assertion that the demonic makes the most fearful appearance when it is the prevailing characteristic of a man. Though not always excellent human beings, personalities of such a disposition exert an incredible influence over mankind.

But the most beautiful expression of the demonic has been given by Goethe in the poem *Urworte. Orphisch*, Primeval Orphic Sayings, the first of which, carrying the title *Dämon*, declares that man is born with his fate and law under a constellation of stars, that he cannot do anything else but live and be in accordance with what the Daimon laid in his nature:

> Wie an dem Tag, der dich der Welt verliehen,
> Die Sonne stand zum Grusse der Planeten,
> Bist alsobald und fort und fort gediehen,
> Nach dem Gesetz wonach du angetreten.
> So musst du seyn, dir kannst du nicht entfliehen,
> So sagten schon Sibyllen, so Propheten;
> Und keine Zeit und keine Macht zerstückelt
> Geprägte Form die lebend sich entwickelt.

> As on the day that brought thee to this earth
> The sun stood in conjunction with the stars,
> So art thou fashioned by the heavenly laws
> That mark thy ways and walk with thee from birth.
> Thus art thou stamped: thyself thou canst not flee.
> Thus spake the Sibyls, thus the Prophets spake.
> Not vastly time nor any power can break
> The living Form that grows eternally.

Now it must be to us of more than a passing interest to see whom Goethe considered to represent the demonic nature, and we shall do well here and there to look into the reason he had for his judgment. Of himself he said that the demonic did not lie in his nature, yet that he was subject to it. On the other hand, he thought Egmont to be the true example of the demonic, although it must be said that the *demonic* Egmont was of the poet's making, rather than the count of history. But among historical figures there appear Byron, Frederick II, Peter the Great of Russia, and many another, and above all Napoleon, whose genius or demon Goethe understood more deeply and before anyone else, despite such exceptional interpretations as those of Görres and Beethoven, each understanding the demonic Napoleon in a different way.

We may be surprised to find that Goethe thought the demonic nature to come into its own more frequently among musicians than among other artists. And yet there is no reason for surprise because Goethe appraised the very nature of music itself to have the demonic as a constituent of its essence. As he imagined the demonic to be transcendent and inaccessible to the intellect or reason, so he surmised that music, high above the world of material things, cannot be approached by reason; nor can its effect, though swaying all, be reasonably accounted for. But on the ground of such characteristics and such an effect we comprehend that the religious cult cannot forego the use of music; for music, according to Goethe, is to be included among the primary means of exerting a marvelous influence upon man. The marvelous, the transcendental, and the mysterious bear witness to the demonic nature of music in consequence of which musicians partake of the demonic to a higher degree than other artists.

Goethe in his conversations with Eckermann once

touched upon the word "composition" and expressed himself in angry terms on the inappropriate use of the word when applied to a work of art. One can "compose" the single parts of a machine made piecemeal, and in such a case the word "composition" is justified. But to speak of an artistic work, an organic entity, as a composition attests to an abominable misuse of the word. "How can one say," Goethe exclaims, "that Mozart *composed* his *Don Giovanni!* A *composition!* as though it were a piece of a cake or a biscuit, with eggs, flour, and sugar mixed together." The work, however, is "the product of the mind, *eine geistige Schöpfung*, with its parts as well as the whole being of *one* spirit, of *one* cast, of *one* breath of life, and when producing his work in no case did the artist experiment, piece together, and proceed arbitrarily; on the contrary, the demonic spirit held his genius in such a powerful grip as to make him execute what it commanded."

Thus did Goethe affiliate Mozart with the demonic musicians, but not alone for the reason that the demonic belonged to music itself. It is, rather, the creative act, the production of an organic form which, issuing from the mysterious energies of the demon, appears in the light of the demonic, and Mozart's work stands as an example of all that the demonic nature of the musician is capable of accomplishing.

One further step will bring us still closer to our subject. Goethe once received a letter from Zelter who reported about a miscarried performance of Handel's *Messiah*, a failure leading Zelter to say that weakness seems to be the characteristic trait of the age. The letter induced Eckermann to express his hope that an adequate music of *Faust* still might see the light of day. In his reply Goethe quickly curbed the vain hope of his partner by deciding firmly and on the spur of the moment that the music of *Faust* had become wholly impossible. And this was his reason: "The forbidding, the disagreeable, the frightful which the music must express at least in part would be contrary to the taste of the time," and Goethe added the remark that "the music of *Faust* should be in the character of *Don Giovanni;* Mozart should have created the music to *Faust.*"

This extraordinary statement, indeed, invites all our imagination to come into play. Goethe certainly did not intend merely to express his great esteem of Mozart; this he had done many a time and by wondrous modulations of his feeling. Nor did he simply give vent to his desire of seeing the music of *Faust* composed somewhat in the style of Mozart. Detached from all external aspects of the matter his judgment must have been based upon the very nature of the music he fancied, and of the musician whom he thought fit for the work. In other words, Goethe must have understood *Don Giovanni* as being a tragedy or at least of tragic character because the demonic disposition impelled Don Giovanni the man to run the fateful course of tragedy; and only a demonic musician such as Mozart would be capable of doing justice to Faust, the demonic and the tragic.

When in our discourse the time will come for us to give our attention to the tragic musician in history, the affinity of the tragic and the demonic will prove itself to have been the chisel with which to cut in relief the fate of many an artist.

So we have reached the end of our survey over the vast scene which the theme "Tragedy in the Art of Music" unfolds before our eyes. Even the first attempt of trying the depth of the theme has shown the implications to be complex and the offshoots to be numerous. The music of Greek tragedy—the spring of all that was to come—and its renaissance in the music drama, the presentation of the tragic in dramatic composition, the afterlife of Greek themes in the opera, the tragédie lyrique, the pathos of the tragic in music, the tragic component of historical situations, tragic figures in history—such are the ramifications of "Tragedy in the Art of Music."

Although it is true that history fraught with the substance of our theme will be the counselor on our road, the thread of Ariadne to guide us through the intricacies of the labyrinth, is it that history alone bears witness to the tragic in music? Does tragedy no longer resound in music and musician of today? Our sense of genuine greatness may be deadened by the noise that nowadays is made of trifles; we probably confuse, more often than not, the tragic issue with any story of misery or a deplorable state of affairs; we are likely to have forgotten "the bliss born of pain"; and we may have become callous to the reverberation of tragedy. Nevertheless, the present situation of the artist and his work is, perhaps, more deeply marked by the tragic than we are ready to admit. Our discourse must conclude with the musician of today.

II

Greek Tragedy

While approaching the subject of Greek tragedy, there comes to my mind the essay "Of Democritus and Heraclitus" by Montaigne, where he speaks of judgment as an instrument he studiously employed whenever faced with subjects of any sort and description. "Tantost je le [jugement] promene à un subject noble et tracassé, auquel il n'a rien à trouver de soy, le chemin en estant si frayé qu'il ne peut marcher que sur la piste d'autruy. Là il fait son jeu à eslire la route quy lui semble la meilleure, et, de mille sentiers, il dict que cettuy-cy, ou celui là, a esté le mieux choisi." In the early seventeenth-century translation by John Florio, rightly famous for its beauty, but not always precise, this reads as follows: "Sometimes I address my judgement and contrive it to a noble and out-worne subject, wherein is nothing found subsisting of it selfe, the high way to it, being so bare-trodden, that it cannot march, but in other steps. There he pleaseth himselfe in chusing the course he thinks best, and a thousand paths sometimes he saith, this or that was best chosen."

These words all too well describe our own situation, by no means one of comfort. Noble our subject surely is, yet with no lesser assurance do we ascertain that it has been broached time after time for centuries past.

What preposterous hope then do we dare cherish in our

minds ever to arrive at a judgment of our own? And, also, is it not true that with the view to the noble subject we must march in the steps of those others who have trodden before along the steeply graded highway? It even seems that all who boldly chose a path all their own were looked upon with utter dismay by most travelers of the habitual main road. And among those who met with such an unfortunate experience the most famous example that we can name undoubtedly is the youthful work of Friedrich Nietzsche, *The Birth of Tragedy out of the Spirit of Music,* the first work he wrote in Basel after having been appointed university professor there at the age of 24. Of this work more must be said presently.

Although we feel ourselves enheartened that despite the nobility of the subject, venerable for its age and greatness, one or another well-chosen way still lies open before us, all our scrupulous efforts of finding the proper access to the subject must appear like wheels that labor in the sand. The music of Greek tragedy being at present our concern, what do we intend to talk about if we must admit at the outset that the very substance, the music itself, no longer exists?

Our task would be quickly disposed of, were it merely to consist in presenting the list of the music that has been preserved. All is lost but a tiny fragment containing no more than some thirty notes. Appearing on the famous Euripides papyrus, probably written between 250 and 150 B.C., it is part of the music for the antistrophe of the first stasimon in the *Orestes* which Euripides is recorded to have composed in 408.

Now, Dionysius of Halicarnassus, who must have owned and examined an original score of the *Orestes,* as shown by his quotation of the chorus in question, reports in the chapter "On Variety" of his work *On Literary Composition:* "The writers of lyric verse cannot vary the melodies of strophe and antistrophe . . . in all the strophes and antistrophes the same sequences must be observed. Nor, again, must the rhythms be changed in which the entire strophes and antistrophes are written, but these too must remain unaltered."

With this in mind we can, though no more than hypothetically and not without controversial results or gaps, apply the antistrophic fragment to the chorus as a whole. But this is all, and it is desperately little.

While the choral fragment of the *Orestes* has been known for many a decade, of late new musical fragments presumably belonging to tragedies have come to light, in part as yet unpublished, which show bits of verses with their music. It has been suggested that they may be the remainder of an anthology to be used by the professional *tragodos*, the tragic singer, like the long-known fragment on the Berlin papyrus, possibly of a tragedy *Ajax*, but not that of Sophocles, which appears as part of an anthology, once called the "Music Lover's Library."

Anthologies of this sort were surely in need when famous singers offered their repertory in public concerts where the great solo arias of Euripides' tragedies seem to have enjoyed perennial popularity. Satyrus of Samos—to name an example—is recorded to have sung, among other tragic pieces, those from the *Bacchae* of Euripides in a concert he gave at Delphi in the second century.

Whatever the purpose of the collections, if they were such, the new fragments of the tragic texts do not fit the contents of any known tragedy.

Within a frame different from that which is set for our

lectures, we should not hesitate to plunge into scrutinizing the fragments minutely with many an interesting detail resulting from a philological study. But here we must employ all our attention upon the essentials of our theme, trying to sift, as it were, the universal from the particular, and it is precisely with the view to the essentials that the absence of the music itself sets painful bounds to the scope of our discussion.

When Friedrich Nietzsche published his first major work in 1871, *The Birth of Tragedy out of the Spirit of Music,* the spark of a genius put the whole clan of philologians aghast. For there was a clear case of a rebellious member who dared affront the sodality of classicists by making his thrust entirely out of line with all accepted procedures. Unheard-of the boldness of his diction, the elated style of which seemed more befitting the lyrical gushes of a poet rather than the abstemious idiom of the scholar; unheard-of the boundless confidence which misled the young author even to the point of disdaining the evidence properly to be given by quoting chapter and verse; and what of the eccentric audacity which enticed him to contaminate the integrity of a historical phenomenon such as Greek tragedy by the association with a product of modern times, the music drama of Richard Wagner, and this for the sole purpose of serving the sorcerer of Bayreuth.

As a retrospective critic sixteen years later Nietzsche freely admitted all the shortcomings of his youthful work. With eyes "more mature, and a hundred times more fastidious, but . . . by no means colder," he looked upon the overwrought style as being "heavy, painful, image-angling and image-entangling" and upon the ideas as being disfigured by formulas of Kant and Schopenhauer. Above all, he recanted the primary sin of his youth, the association with Richard Wagner who made him hide the Greek theme "even under the bad manners of the Wagnerian." "I spoiled the grand Hellenic problem, as it had opened up before me, by the admixture of the most modern things. That I entertained hopes, where nothing was to be hoped for, where everything pointed all-too-clearly to an approaching end!" Free from the distorting shackles of Wagnerianism, such was the worthiest result that issued from his late appraisal. But as regards the mainspring of his thought, the principle of his adventure, he remained steady, without remorse or recantation.

What was at the core of his bold enterprise? The discovery that both the origin and the nature of the tragedy, even of the tragic on the whole, were kindled by the god Dionysus; that tragic music was essentially Dionysian; that the rise and fall of Greek tragedy were hinged to the unflagging power of the myth; that the tragedy as a work of art came into being by the confluence of the Apollonian and the Dionysian, and that the union of the two gods procreated the substance of a new aesthetic judgment untrammeled by the pursuit of moral guilt and sin. Though it was the art work of pessimism, Greek tragedy proved, even to the satisfaction of the historian, that pessimism did not toll the bells of a declining age; rather, it emerged as the token of Greek culture at its fullest, while the optimistic views of life, the trust of Socrates in the effectiveness of scientific knowledge, the celebrated cheerfulness or serenity of the Greeks, were nothing but the last rays of the "glowing sunset" of Hellenism. The tragedy, however, rose to being the most Hellenic manifestation of a glorious pessimism "Beyond Good and Evil."

That Greek tragedy, springing as it apparently did from the old dithyramb, the Bacchanalian song, "was originally only chorus, and nothing but chorus," could hardly be upheld as a discovery of something unknown; and Nietzsche laid no claim to the originality of the assertion.

But he disburdened the problem of the tragic chorus from various misconceptions which had been dearly nursed by many a scholar of classical studies. He turned away from the political notion that the chorus of the tragedy acted as though it were a "constitutional representation" of the democratic Athenians. And he flung himself, angrier still, at the fanciful opinion that the chorus performed the part of the "ideal spectator," a concept which—I venture to say— walked around like a never dying ghost ever since August Wilhelm Schlegel had ushered it into the world of letters.

Why should the chorus be considered a spectator, to forget all about its being an ideal one? Did the ancient chorus not consist at first of creatures in the disguise of satyrs? Did it not appear originally as an actor, the main actor, rather than as a spectator? If the chorus is the prime actor of the *tragodia*, the tragic song, and is supposed at the same time to be the ideal spectator, the tragedy would have no play at all, and Nietzsche rightly flouted at the absurdity of having the spectator without the play.

Although the thesis that tragedy was a descendant of the chorus of satyrs had been a long established intelligence, it suddenly became resplendent again by being cast into the full glare of a new light. Not the initial thesis but the inference deduced from it gave rise to the startling idea that tragedy was born from the spirit of music.

Now, Nietzsche did not assert such a strange birth merely on the grounds that at all times music had been allotted a substantial though varying share in Greek tragedy. Even the capacity of the chorus as the sole actor in consequence of which the tragic text must have been sung throughout, even this complete concurrence of music and text in the earliest phase, did not bear heavily upon the main idea. Not the mere presence of music, but its spirit determined his philosophy.

The significance which he detected in the chorus of satyrs and jointly in the Dionysian element of the tragedy mysteriously mingled with the spirit of music. The Dionysian revelers, "with their frame flooded by the god in his fullness," reconciled themselves to nature and in a state of ecstasy experienced the "oneness with the primal source of the universe," forfeit but recaptured when possessed by the god. So also were the satyrs, the companions of Dionysus, "fictitious natural beings," yet recognized as real when seen on the stage as if they were to testify to a long forgotten past when man and nature still embraced each other in a cosmic harmony. And Nietzsche brilliantly declared that "the satyr, as being the Dionysian chorist, lives in a religiously acknowledged reality under the sanction of the myth and cult."

As astounding a phenomenon as the rise of tragedy from the chorus must represent itself symbolically: the satyr—the initiator—became the mouthpiece of the Dionysian wisdom that man, led back to the heart of nature, returned, as it were, to Paradise Lost. The tragedy transmitted this wisdom as a consolation that life despite all its destructive changes remained "indestructibly powerful and joyful" with the satyric chorus making the consolation appear in the flesh, tangible and visible. No degree of sophistication, the accessory to all highly developed civilizations, was capable of wiping out the human trust in the primeval alliance of man with the elements of nature.

The original chorus then was nothing but "a self-mirroring of the Dionysian man," and when it came in sight in the orchestra of the theater it re-established its oneness with Dionysus. To this I may do well to add that the Athenians were constantly reminded of the presence of the god and of the sacrificial rites by the altar placed in the middle of the circular orchestra in the Dionysian theater at Athens, where the so-called City Dionysia were celebrated in the month of March with the competitive performance of the dramas being a major part of the spring festivals. Viewing the altar and the chorus, the Greek, an enchanted Dionysian reveler, saw himself as a satyr, and as a satyr he in turn "beheld the god."

It is here that the concept of the satyric chorus merged in the spirit of music, the Dionysian music of the tragedy. Together with the appearance of the satyrs the Dionysian musician re-echoed the primordial pain and joy, the suffering and the exultation, the tragic and the ecstatic, in the service of the god whom the old dithyramb never failed to invoke. Because of his Dionysian nature the musician produced "the copy of the primordial unity *as music*," "granting," so Nietzsche continued, "that music has been correctly termed a repetition and a recast of the world." Now the notion of music as a repetition of the world had its very roots in the philosophy of music which Schopenhauer evolved in *The World as Will and Representation*.

There music occupied a place of distinction all its own and entirely apart from all the other arts. For Schopenhauer contrived musical expressions to be analogous to concepts because both were related in like manner to the world of phenomena, and he ascertained that concepts are the "universalia post rem" as they are abstractions from things, that music gives the "universalia ante rem" which are prior to all things real, while the "universalia in re" represent the world of reality. Hence music could be said to be a repetition of the world, an antecedent of reality, and an image of primordial elements.

If, according to Schopenhauer, music "gives the innermost kernel preceding all form, or the heart of things," and if, according to Nietzsche, Dionysian music mirrors a primordial state of unity in the life of man, then, but only then, we should be ready to admit that the Dionysian musician, forever re-creating the myth indispensable to Greek tragedy, produces the "universalia ante rem." Then, indeed, the spirit of music, the Dionysian spirit, has given birth to tragedy.

Such an admission, however, cannot but purport a certain acquiescence on philosophic grounds, as though we were to yield for a moment to a conclusion logically drawn from given preliminaries. The response must needs be altogether different if we should contemplate the position of Nietzsche on strictly historical grounds. But there the trouble starts. A philologian of the rare hue which blends the artistic imagination with the scientific mind, Nietzsche most naturally conceived Greek tragedy within the confines of a historical problem. But the drift of genius carried the philologian into the province of philosophy where the metamorphosis of thought transformed a historical theme into a comprehensively human problem of universal significance. It is not for the first time, nor for the last, that history and philosophy confronted each other face to face with irreconcilable hostility. Not only the bias toward Richard Wagner but also the ambition of reaching absolute—that is,

philosophic—conclusiveness tarnished the integrity of th
historical thought. And yet, if stripped of all the effects
which followed bias or philosophy, there still remains a
notable portion of the historical argument which for all its
daring novelty stands the severe test of philological scrutiny.

In the first place, the simple statement of Aristotle that
tragedy began with the improvisations allied to the singing
of the dithyramb was brought to bear upon unsuspected
implications which, lifted into the light of their inherent
context, showed all of a sudden the musical framework of
the early tragedy. And what Nietzsche asserted for the
primitive form of drama subsisted to a large measure at
least in the tragedy of Aeschylus. In the second place, irre-
spective of the inspiring exuberance, so often the guileful
pilot to juvenescent, hence pardonable, exaggeration, Nietzsche forcefully instilled a new energy into the inquiry
about the Dionysian problem. Even the most recent studies
on Dionysus, his myth and cult, owe not a little to the
impulse of Nietzsche.

Although we shall not easily find his peer, we must render
honor to a precursor who is in importance to our theme his
equal: Paul Graf York von Wartenburg, whose essay on
the catharsis of Aristotle and Sophocles' *Oedipus at Colonus*
appeared five years prior to the work of Nietzsche. A
towering figure among gentlemen-scholars, Count York,
mainly known by his correspondence with Wilhelm Dil-
they, set a stunning example of uncommon erudition. Like
Nietzsche's work on the birth of the tragedy, York's
"Catharsis" is the product of a youthful scholar. But in
contrast to Nietzsche, a classical philologist by profession,
Count York could lay no claim to any of the securities professional scholarship may or may not grant its disciples; and

...natched all the dexterities of avocation.
...he temptation of seeing into the singular
...nonprofessional scholar, we must abide by
...erms of our theme.

...know, two men of letters, historians of philos-
...been struck by a curious recurrence of York's
...in the work of Nietzsche, who never named his
...sor although the sameness of ideas extended at
times almost to literal quotations. Both these scholars were discouraged by what they took to be a total lack of documentary evidence that Nietzsche had really known the study of Count York.

Moreover, the apodictic declaration issued by Elizabeth Förster, the sister of Nietzsche—as high-handed a guardian of the Nietzsche Archives in Weimar as the autocratic lady at the rival court in Wagnerian Bayreuth—that Nietzsche could not possibly have known the work of York seems to have closed all further questioning. Yet that little, perhaps not even excusable, vanity accessory to professional scholarship persuades me to report that the university library at Basel still keeps the records of the books which Nietzsche borrowed. And there it is in black and white that he had studied the publication of his elder. The fact that he omitted any mention of his source of inspiration, in no way detrimental to the merits of his own discovery, may be explained by his surrender to the philosophy of Schopenhauer and Wagner, who forced him into a region far remote from the climate of York's essay.

But is there any need for us to go the full length of discussing the theses of Nietzsche and York? It will perhaps be remembered that one of the avenues traced for our approach to Greek tragedy should lead us to the Dionysian nature of tragic music. Written in the lofty style that rises to the same level with the loftiness of thought without which even scholarship will have no lasting consequence, the study of York unlocked another Dionysian secret of Greek music. And wholly different from the position of Nietzsche, Count York insisted emphatically upon the historical character of the problem. He placed it in the midst of the question at issue: the catharsis brought about as the ultimate attainment of Greek tragedy.

The famous definition that tragedy must produce—by way of pity, or, better, compassion and fear, or, better, terror—a catharsis, a purification of alike passions or affections, presented by Aristotle almost casually in his *Poetics*, gave in fact more trouble than enlightenment. In addition, Aristotle maintained that a certain joyful feeling should lie within the final effect. No wonder that ceaseless efforts were engaged to solve the riddle of having the affections, *pathemata*, of terror and compassion result in something in the nature of joyful serenity.

The catharsis has stirred the minds of many a man ever since the days of the renascent Greek drama, and especially during the sixteenth and seventeenth centuries, the great age when theoretical discussions flourished. As a result the explications of the Aristotelian text, defective as it is, even if not tampered with, are legion merely to remain controversial up to the present time.

As no one reasonably can be expected to take the risk of wading through a torrent of amassed opinions, Count York would shrink from any such attempt. But happily he rescued the tragic catharsis from misapprehensions, of which no other seems to have done greater harm than the moral interpretation based on the concept of guilt. Let it be noted that as much as guilt, the outcome of action in consequence of a personal character, and moral justice, the sequel of wrongdoing, might mark the peculiarities of the drama in modern times, both concepts were foreign to Greek tragedy. And I should say further that with a view to ancient drama English-speaking writers have consistently avoided the term "guilt"; instead, they talk of the "tragic flaw." But though the minor defect which Aristotle assumed to blemish the hero of the tragedy can be defined, most adequately indeed, as a flaw, the great *hamartia*, another of the Aristotelian requisites, which is translated by Germans as "guilt" or "sin," does not fit the connotation of a flaw. Whatever else the murder of Laius by Oedipus or the murder of Clytemnestra by her son Orestes may be, they certainly are not flaws or errors of judgment.

Keeping the moral criterion away from any aspect of Greek tragedy, Count York put the catharsis to the touch of the Dionysian arbiter. The religious service, rendered to Dionysus, *ho lysios*, the divine deliverer, culminated in the state of ecstasy which enhanced the affections of pain and exuberance, of terror and compassion, to the point of mutual balance, that is, to the point of deliverance. By the same token, the tragedy would attain its peak in the ultimate cleansing of the affections, in the ecstatic catharsis, the twin congenial to the ritual lustration. The tragic catharsis would, therefore, reveal the vestige of religion. To speak with the words of Count York, the tragedy appeared to be "nothing less than the transfigured Bacchic rite, a higher potency of the Dionysian cult." And the spur of the Dionysian music penetrating both the cult and the drama to the same depth and with the same substance provoked the state of religious ecstasy as it impelled the tragic catharsis.

It now would seem that the famous passages on music

which Aristotle included in the eighth book of his *Politics* might lend themselves with enough strength to clinch the argument. Many a time they have been solicited for the support of one theory or another, and each time they yield whatever might favor any school of thought.

When classifying the various melodies according to their character, Aristotle spoke of the orgiastic, the enthusiastic, even the cathartic melos, allied now to the tragic affections of terror and compassion, now to the ritual ecstasy. Instead of bringing new pressure upon a text which says too little to grant explicit evidence and yet too much to keep the curiosity of mind at rest, we should insist that the ambiguity, as fluctuating as it always is, does not reflect the weakness of the definition; it lies rather in the nature of the orgiastic, cathartic music itself which parcels out its power between the drama and the cult. And when Aristotle referred to the aulos, the property of which he specified as orgiastic to the exclusion of shaping the *ethos*, the character, a state of ethics, he strongly advised that the instrument should be employed only upon the occasion of performances which aim at the catharsis rather than at *mathesis*, knowledge, instruction. Performances of what? Of the drama or the rite where orgiastic music played its legitimate part. Indeed, when the chorus made its solemn appearance on the stage ready to sing the parodos of the drama, it was headed by the aulos player adorned with the *ritual* attire of the station he held in the *religious* cult, and with this apparel, different from that of the chorus, the aulos player beckoned Dionysus upon the stage.

Since our knowledge of Greek tragedy begins with the complete and perfect drama of Aeschylus, it cannot but be that all the musical constituents of the tragedy, compared with an imaginary primitive phase, were pregnant with symbolic meaning, at once artistically elaborate and refined to the utmost; and each symbolic purport must have been like a thread woven to tie the musical elements to the religious implications of the origin—thus to tie it to something that had passed away and yet was still alive.

The old dithyramb, which shed tragedy as an offspring destined to take flight into a world of its own, no longer existed as a choral song danced in honor of the god Dionysus. But at the Dionysian festivals the new dithyramb, completely estranged from its ancestor, though carrying the same name improperly suggestive of kinship, was nonetheless a part of the musical competition at the side of the competitive dramas.

On the whole then, without the exemplary symbolic significance, the music of tragedy could never have come close to the task it was appointed to fulfill; nor would the spectator, the listener, ever have been in a position better than that of grappling tediously but vainly with the incomprehensible portent of the music. Are we really to believe in the light of such fruitless toils that Aristotle claimed the music to have been held by the spectator as the most impressive or the most attractive among the essential components of tragedy? Surely, he might have thought of the musical effect as being one of a bewitching entertainment, and in his own day the dazzling display of tricks and twists by the virtuoso soloist might have been, more often than not, the chief reason for the audience to be sensationally regaled. When in his *Poetics* he indicated the extraordinary position of music in the tragedy, he hardly had in mind such lavish dexterities of craftsmanship, so often the token that more and more substance had drained off from underneath a brilliant surface. At the very outset, he ranked the element of music high among the essentials effecting the drama by the force of *mimesis,* of which our own word "imitation" is at best an inadequate, if not a cruelly misleading, translation.

There were but two agents which performed the imitation: the exquisite verbal expression, that is, the art of versification; and the music auxiliary in developing the poetic art to the full-blown power of its being. Both the poetic art and the music must needs serve the object of imitation: they imitate the myth presented in the artistic shapes of action.

But here we are hard pressed by the narrow limits of what the word "imitation" implies or may imply. If we speak of imitative music, we immediately have before our mind a realistic copy of visual associations; we imagine the music to imitate the waves of the ocean, the throbbing voice of the nightingale, the martial sounds of battle; we think of tonal pictures, of program music, and the like. Now, such realistic, imitative music, both instrumental and vocal, had its day of fashion among the Greeks; it also intruded into the drama, as Timotheus is reported to have included in his *Persians* the musical presentation of the battle of Salamis whereby he must have broken music on the wheel of torture; and the "ant crawls" or the warbling sounds in the composition of Agathon which Aristophanes derided no doubt belong to the same type of music made of fustian.

Although we must admit these ravings of artistic fancy to range within the bounds of imitation, we still maintain that in the understanding of Aristotle, the *mimesis* of old, the maker of the drama, had been an imitation more symbolic than realistic. But symbolism must fall short of being comprehended unless style, convention, and tradition are attuned to one accord.

Now, confronted with the assurance gathered from

sources of various description, all the means of musical expression which came to bear upon the *mimesis* betokened the virtues of style, convention, and tradition by both their nature and their action: the choice of the key in which the song is to be rendered, the *harmonia*, the mode; the shift from the median to the high or low range of the voice; the meter and the rhythm with every device of a fluctuating tempo; the recitative, that is, the form found midway between song and speech; the choice of the instrument, of the aulos or the cithara; the structure of the lyric chorus, at least in part bound up with the tradition of the cult; the shape of the kommos, the dirge, the song of lament related to the chorus; and last but not least, the style of melody in the elaborate soloistic aria as well as in the choral lyrics.

But does this inventory of musical contrivances really testify to the coherence which we expect the style to grant? In face of the fact that the music of tragedy changed its appearance at least three times in the quick course of but one century, can it be that tradition, the memory of man, "runneth not to the contrary"? Yet style and tradition are never equivalent to a sterile conservatism unless they have lost all vital meaning.

If we admire Aeschylus as the most jealous keeper of tradition, this must mean but one thing: that in form and even more in spirit his tragedy was closest to the roots of origin; in form, because the choral lyrics, hence the music reigned over the very shape of the dramatic work; and in spirit, because the chorus, always responsive and obedient to the divine ordinance of fate, sheltered the obligation to religion.

Did Aeschylus betray himself and the tradition when, late in his life and possibly under the pressure of the younger generation, he yielded to the modern trend and granted the solo song a vaster expanse than it ever had before in any of his tragedies? Despite the acceptance of a novelty, if acceptance it was, Aeschylus formed the new fashion in accordance with his own conceptions. Never detached from the choral partner, the soloist, like the choral leader, evolved the song by means of the closest correspondence with the chorus. When Cassandra sings her ominous song in alternation with the chorus she trembles with the divine frenzy of prophetic vision. Her song, though bearing witness to a novelty of music, remains enthralled by the religious fervor of old.

Of the tragedians, Euripides, esteemed by Aristotle as the most tragic dramatist, seems to have departed farthest from the course of the tradition. Indeed, he humbled the chorus to the function of an intermezzo disengaged from the action; he nearly relinquished the intercourse between the chorus and the soloist, skillfully constructing, in its stead, elaborate arias by taking the musical characteristics of the new dithyramb as a model. 1287195

The musical composition, the aria, served one purpose only, but one of far-reaching consequence: the expression of human passion and despair. The violence of passion and the madness that "burneth to chant its song, and leap and rave," though still effusions of the Dionysian spirit, now cast off the remnants of the cult. With every tangible trace of the religious tradition effaced, the chant was but the passionate recital of human suffering, ecstasy without the god. And yet, as if for fear lest ill betide, Euripides paid his last tribute, *The Bacchae*, to the god Dionysus, to the origin of the tragedy.

III

Music Drama Reborn

The rebirth of music drama proffers a tale, by no means always glorious, yet never failing to inspire those capable of listening with confidence to the utterances of fancy, a story of twofold significance. For that which saw the light of day anew had submerged aforetime in the great deep of oblivion with but a ripple on the surface betokening the presence of the sunken treasures. This is as much a story of forgotten-ness as it is a story of remembrance.

The artisan among historians, a devotee to the belief in cause and effect and hence in the unbroken continuity of historical evolution, will take the force of human memory to be the strongest element of history, and if he finds no cause memorized, he sees no effect.

When the rebirth of the music drama came to pass, the very object said to be reborn had been erased from the memory of man for centuries past. Whatever buried treas-ures were ultimately rescued, the teeth of time had gnawed away the once inseparable companion, music, from all the remnants of the drama. If we admit, as we surely must, Greek tragedy to have been a music drama, the torso which survived could not but be an unremitting challenge to the fancy of the musician, with little guidance and no model to pilot the attempt of restoration.

Faced with appalling gaps in the story of survival and

watching the musician re-create a music he had never heard, the historian often seeks in vain to string the effects, that is, the music drama reborn, on the thread of causes recorded of Greek tragedy. No matter how relaxed the stricture of the bonds between the offspring and its parent might have been, it still was narrow enough for the offspring at least imaginatively to aspire toward the condition of the parent, the drama of antiquity.

We cannot be content with the thought that the complete loss of the music set to Greek tragedy deprived the restorer of any claim to being the legitimate architect of an authentic reconstruction. The fervor of his belief, buttressed by only scanty knowledge, could have been no more real if all the remnants of history had escaped the wrecks and scars of time. It is the indisputable privilege of the artist to have his fancy roam within the limits of its realm even if the limits lie above or below those of past ages. No work of art has its ultimate justification in history or historical tradition, and if the history of art has strangely been said to be the history of revivals, at least with equal right it can also be said that it is the history of things forgotten, discontinued, and forsaken.

It would appear that the story of survival began at a time when Greek tragedy was suffering from the woes and aches of declining age. Wrapped in a nearly impenetrable shroud of obscurity, tragedy subsequent to Euripides no longer can be pieced together into an intelligible whole, and what we know of its characteristics flows from literary criticism rather than from works of art, from such criticism as Aristophanes produced on the stage. Still, the work of Euripides, lasting through the decline and disintegration of Greek culture, lived far into the Hellenistic period and much longer than the work of any other tragedian. This is no doubt partly because of its popularity, so curiously puzzling as the increasingly vulgar taste of the theatrical audience clamored rather for artistic currency debased, and partly because the stream of creative energies ceased at last to bring new tragedies to the theater.

We do not know at what time all came to a close, sucking even Euripides' tragedies into the whirlpools of decay. Whatever slender popularity may have lingered on, it did not save the drama from becoming a thing of the past, although Greek tragedy did imprint at least its trace—and again it is the trace of Euripides rather than of Aeschylus or Sophocles—upon Latin drama.

If in speaking of ancient drama we have in mind Greek tragedy, we must admit that the rude storms of history swept it entirely out of sight for centuries to come. If we concede that Greek tragedy bequeathed at least some of its attainments to Latin drama, then Greek tragedy may be said to have had a sequel.

And it is but one, Seneca, who has the claim to being an heir to the Greek tragedians. Yet what had become of a heritage that the heir no longer was capable of conducting in the sense of the bequest. Not only was tragedy stripped of the vestment with which the Dionysian festivals adorned it, the tragedies of Seneca were entirely removed from the stage of the ancient theater. They were written to be read by those who believed in the blissful sustenance of the craving mind, and none of the tragedies of Seneca ever appeared on stage. Nevertheless, whatever immediate information on ancient drama the Middle Ages possessed was gathered from the tragedies of Seneca. Not that they were mounted at long last upon the stage; they remained what they were at the time of Seneca: literary works to be read or at best to be recited. Likewise the Roman comedies of Terence and Plautus, by far the unrivaled favorites throughout the Middle Ages, appertained to the stock of instructive material for recitation in schools to the benefit of rhetorical eloquence.

Tightly laced by stringent bonds, the sense of tragedy and the feeling for the tragic consequently shrank to the slenderest measure among the artistic experiences medieval men were able to draw from antiquity. Even from the theoretical sources on tragedy very little issued rich enough to expand the limits of knowledge and to nurture the sense of the tragic. And of that little, a good deal appeared to be encumbered with the burden of freakish polemics in the name of religion as the debate on the tragedy swiftly turned round to question the merits of ancient poetry on the whole and to cast blame upon the immorality of the ancient theater.

If freed from all the distorting polemics, not much is left to account for the theoretical intelligence of Greek tragedy. Probably best known throughout the Middle Ages was the definition Isidore of Seville gave of the *tragodoi*, the singers of tragedy, who—in his words—sang the old stories to the spectators, sang of the deeds of criminal kings in a lugubrious poem. And quite general was the belief that tragic works always dealt with public affairs as well as the stories of kings or men of dignified station, while the arguments of the tragedies always consisted of doleful subjects. This definition, handed down in part or in full from one generation to the other, even survived the Middle Ages.

Of all the Aristotelian works, the *Poetics*, surely the main theoretical source on tragedy, did not leave any deep marks upon the medieval mind; apparently least known, it also was least commented upon. Like other works of Aristotle it was transmitted to the western world by way of Arabian translations. So Averroës (d. 1198) paraphrased the *Poetics*, which must have caused him considerably more trouble than the rest of the Aristotelian opus.

Though this is not the time to dwell upon the historical significance of the paraphrase, we must not eschew the definition of tragedy which Averroës rendered by extending the Aristotelian text in a manner marked for its own. He deemed the tragedy the best art of praise (*Optima ars laudandi, id est Tragoedia*), which, by way of metrical speech, that is, in verse, imitates things prominent, action illustrious, voluntary, and perfect, whereby compassion and terror (*misericordia et terror*) move the human mind to the right affection (*affectio recta*); and this comes about, from dispositions conducive to virtues, when imitating upright men by means of holiness and purity (*sanctitas et puritas*). So all-important did the moral purpose appear to Averroës that he labored the argument to the utmost of his exertion, trying to probe compassion and terror for the faculty of spurring man to emulate virtue and refrain from wickedness. And when he went about to illustrate his argument he, significantly enough, chose the biblical stories of Joseph and his brothers as well as of Abraham and the sacrifice of Isaac rather than the mythical stories of antiquity. Although fully aware that the tragedy according to Aristotle must lead ultimately to compassion and terror, Averroës turned the ancient meaning end for end so thoroughly that, truly, the final result of the tragedy became the moral purpose of serving the betterment of mankind. The complete change of meaning invited the moral motives to be the sole judges with no artistic criterion to mitigate the severity of the judgment passed on the delinquent, the tragic drama.

If want of knowledge can be held responsible for the shrinkage of the feeling for the tragic, moral judgment certainly must be counted among the causes which brought the medieval men close to rejecting tragedy altogether, to an antagonism toward the tragic. Stories such as those of Orestes, Oedipus, Medea, or Atys naturally were well known. But what usefulness could ever lie in telling the stories of incest, homicide, castration, or rape? This question was actually raised and encouraged by reading the literature of the Church Fathers, of Tertullian, of Augustine, even of pagan writers such as Plutarch, Lucian, or Martial, and the practices of the late Roman theater, recorded by many an author, added to the feeling of fright and disgust. With Fate in the Greek sense being relinquished, nothing but sheer horror remained. No wonder it was suggested that instead of reading the story of Oedipus or of Thyestes, one should better read what life itself can say, that tragic misery as a reality of life should be more attentively looked into than the misery of mythological stories. No wonder, with nothing but repulsiveness and odious horror thought to be the characteristics of ancient tragedy, that medieval men—and Dante one of them—understood the *tragos*, the goat from which tragedy derived, to portray the drama most faithfully as an animal, in front a splendid sight, but mean and hideous from behind, offensive its odor and ugly its voice, the very goat song, the *tragodia*.

In the light of this outspoken aversion we can understand why no tragedy ever took shape as a work of art during the Middle Ages though conceptions such as those we singled out survived and passed over into the epoch of the Renaissance. And another notion was saved from the wreckage of time: the intelligence that tragedy, always sung, had always been a music drama.

Yet did the Middle Ages truly fail in shaping the tragic? What of the sacred drama? Do the dramatic representations of biblical stories or legends of martyrs really lie outside the scope of tragedy? And above all, is the passion play, the drama of Christ's suffering and pain, not the sum and substance of any tragedy that ever came to pass? But all sacred dramas, including the passion play—remarkably late in its appearance among medieval plays—were not only the outgrowth of the liturgy, but were part of the liturgical service within the church. And all services had but one purpose: *glorificatio Dei et edificatio hominum,* the glorification of God and the edification of men. Glorifying God or edifying men might alleviate the heavy burden of life, but it could never be of tragic nature.

However piercing the impact of Christ's sacrifice in the shape of liturgy might be, however pitiful the story of his passion, there cannot be a tragedy where the redemption of sinful mankind determines the religious meaning of the sacrifice, of suffering and death. As remote from tragedy and from an artistic concept of the tragic as Christ's passion and the salvation of the faithful are the dramas based on the legends of martyrs. Likewise linked to the liturgy, they are the exercise of devotion designed to blaze abroad the power of faith and the glory of heavenly reward. Despite the description of martyrdom, of pain and torture, "the blood of the martyrs is the seed of the church."

The sacred drama thus being a religious service precludes the aesthetic effect as a primary aim, and the liturgical chants which embellish the service are not contrived artistically to express the suffering of martyrdom. Not an artistic bent, but religious edification, a devotional purpose, justifies the liturgical play. This may be a drama in the sense of action, but it is not a tragedy as an independent work of art, and none of the medieval thinkers seems ever to have designated the liturgical drama a tragedy of the ancient fabric by reason of its contents or any fatal event.

Yet some of the themes basic to the sacred drama, Christ's passion first of all, came to be a deep source of inspiration for numerous composers—and the most renowned among them—to render the story of eternal dignity in such tragic tones as no musician prone to shape a tragedy could ever be expected to surpass.

With the Middle Ages thus having lost sight of the ancient tragedy as well as a kindred understanding of the tragic texture, the medieval story of the drama speaks of oblivion rather than of survival, of abandonment rather than of recovery. For the music drama to be reborn, the lost dramatic art had first to be reconquered. This hardly would come within reach unless fresh motives awakened new aspirations.

When Albertino Mussato, the erudite humanist at Padua, resolutely put his efforts into the revival of ancient tragedy, that is, into re-creating a tragic drama of his own, he seems to have released the forces capable of casting about for a new form of the drama. And when his Latin tragedy *Eccerinis* or *Ezzelino* saw the light of day, the year of its recital, 1314, was extolled for having hailed the tragic drama to Italy. And yet, the model for his tragedy was still none other than Seneca, though for the sake of organizing the drama and shaping the dramatic verse he regretted not knowing Greek drama.

In contrast to his Roman model he chose the subject not from ancient myth, but from contemporary history of vital concern to his own home town, Padua. At the same time, the crimes and cruelties of Ezzelino, still fresh in the minds of his fellow citizens, allowed him to present the very specimen of what he, too, supposed a tragedy to be: a gruesome story of vile tyranny, of human vice, and unsurpassed depravity. Though his attempts to be faithful to the formal elements of his model failed to reach the art of Seneca in many a respect, the place and function of the chorus came closest to the Roman tragedy. But even more, Mussato could not escape the impact of the medieval concept; for with the moral proclaimed in the final chorus—that God, a judge both severe and mild, rewards the good as he condemns the evil—the humanistic author fell victim to the doctrine of moral justice which is alien to ancient drama. Yet, in another respect, the *Ezzelino* did not deviate from Seneca. Mussato designed his drama as a literary work to be read, but not to be presented on the stage. Graced with the solemn ceremonies of an academic event in accordance with the ancient custom of reciting poetry in public, the *Ezzelino* was presented to an audience of erudite humanists. All its parts must have been recited; we can muster no evidence that the chorus was chanted.

The event was celebrated as though it were a beacon of hope for the drama to embark afresh upon a course which, if retraced, might lead to the tragic art of old. The hope of reaching the ambitious goal did not seem to be dimmed by the thought that there would be need of gifts more divine than those erudition can grant. Despite the enthusiastic response to the drama of Mussato, the humanist did not inspire the Italian poets further to pursue the skills of the dramatic art. With no successor prompted to step in, the challenge of Mussato was an empty sound, and for this and other reasons we assume that his voice rang like the last echo of a dying time, rather than like the herald of things to come.

Nearly two centuries elapsed until a new tragedy came into being, and now in the vernacular, in Italian rather than in Latin. Mussato's drama had been long forgotten. But new resources were meanwhile discovered by the great humanists of fifteenth-century Italy. And this time there could be no mistake that a new spirit had quickened the advent of new riches. The recovery of Greek manuscripts—the message of ancient literature which included the dramas of the three great tragedians—the rise of Greek scholarship, and the enthusiastic endeavor of conveying the Greek world of letters to the West by both translations and commentaries is a story which, though often told, can never be narrated without exuberance; for it is the story of bringing the western mind home again "to the glory that was Greece."

Around 1500 Aldo, the famous publisher in Venice who wrote for himself a page of lasting merits in the annals of learning, edited the Greek tragedies of Sophocles and Euripides, with an edition of Aeschylus to follow. All of this appeared to have a strange effect upon the Greek scholars, strange because the humanists were slow or cautious in engaging in the formidable task of translation, just as they seem to have shown an initial reluctance toward most of Greek poetry. Or did the reasons for their caution perhaps reach downward into deeper grounds? Must the tragic drama first conquer the Italian stage? Or else, did hesitation come from being disinclined for tragedy? The question must be raised again.

In the midst of the humanistic movement young Angelo Poliziano wrote his *Favola d'Orfeo* for a performance in Mantua in 1471 (or 1472). It is here for the first time that the ancient theme of Orpheus appeared dramatically shaped with music intervening in the form of solo song and chorus. The story drawn from Ovid would clearly place the *Orfeo* into the category of pastoral drama, but not of tragedy. Such was at least the conception of most poets who rendered the theme as a drama. Yet the matter, less simple than it seems, does not rest there. The sudden death of Eurydice and, after having been rescued from Hades, the final death caused by a "tragic flaw" of Orpheus himself bear the mark of the tragic. Poliziano even took from the ancient myth the savage slaying of Orpheus by the Maenads who, with the head of Orpheus torn to pieces, sing at the end of the drama a bacchic dithyramb. This final scene, often omitted by dramatists, usually has been excluded by musicians from their operas, save for Stravinsky who, after having shown the act of slaying, closed his ballet with the apotheosis of Orpheus.

Should Poliziano's play, this *Favola d'Orfeo*, which—with the fateful Maenads of the tragedy and with the dithyramb of the tragic god Dionysus—meets, however accidentally, the Greek spirit of the tragic, be aligned with the pastoral drama? It is at best a hybrid, and even contemporaries were obviously doubtful; for when Antonio Tebaldeo some twenty years later reshaped the work of Poliziano, he named the revised drama *Orphei tragedia*, without having added any new component of a tragic disposition.

Such a want of assurance in ranking dramatic works as the revision revealed subsisted throughout the Renaissance, partly because of the dearth of experience in dramatic composition, but partly also because of the strange apprehensiveness of the tragic. Often, indeed, we are at a loss when searching after the reason for naming a dramatic work a tragedy. Any deplorable event, and surely that of unfortunate love, might justify the name of old distinction. At times, the author himself expressed regret for having been the messenger of a sad story and he dismissed his spectators or readers with the advice not to take the story too seriously, or with the pious wish that nothing so deplorable should ever become their own lot. Or, the dramatist presented "una Tragedia/ in rima/ In toscha lingua con *leggiadri accenti*," a tragedy rhymed in Tuscan language with accents gracefully lighthearted as though the *leggiadri accenti* must needs alleviate the heavy anxieties aroused by the tragedy. Or, the author rendered the outcome of the drama more "lieto" than "mesto" or "tragico," more joyful than mournful, which led to the hybrid name of a "tragicomedia."

The discovery of the Greek plays, the difficulties of which called for many a comment, the intensified study of the drama as a work of art, and finally a new approach of Aristotle's *Poetics* and other ancient sources of like nature would seem to have cleared the way for a more adequate comprehension of the dramatic categories although it did not eliminate inconsistency on the part of the poets. But the question remains whether all this contributed to a new concept of tragedy among Italian dramatists.

For the first time Greek drama was in a position to rival the venerable Seneca, who alone had transmitted to the poet all that was to be known about tragedy. Giangiorgio Trissino, having completed his *Sofonisba* in 1515, could pride himself on having given his countrymen the first Italian tragedy and at the same time the first that might be testimonial to the most precious fruit Greek erudition, or scholarship in general, could ever bear: to be among the incentives of artistic energies. It is true, Trissino sharpened the tools of the dramatist's craft, with Greek tragedy being the new master of the guild; it is true that he emulated Euripides in organizing the scheme of dramatic composition, the episodes, the dialogue and monologue, and the chorus, with the technique of the dramatic verse needful of an adaptation to the nature of the Italian language. But device kept as device makes its presence painfully felt, and only the unblessed among the artists treasure devices when they speak of art. Trissino may well be said to have been a shrewd technician, a deft maker of tools, and for his skills he has the claim to honorable mention in the records of history. But unforgivable would be the error of judgment were we to look upon his *Sofonisba* as the proud offspring of Euripides, or even one of Seneca, or as a tragedy of lasting merits. If merits there are, they all lie within the craft of dramatic technique. And it is not without significance that the influence of the *Sofonisba* was restricted almost entirely to matters technical which, naturally enough, whetted the appetite for debate among the humanists. Even the theatrical practice of the Renaissance failed to be impressed by the *Sofonisba*, and when Trissino's drama, half a century after its completion, was put on the stage for the first time, it did not owe the production to its artistic value, but to the patriotism of the citizens of Vicenza.

Trissino had his share in developing the technique of the

renascent tragedy, but Giovanni Battista Giraldi Cinzio probably contributed most to defining the character of the tragedy by the nature of its contents. His *Orbecche* set the pattern for the concept of the tragic which remained a marked feature of the drama in the Renaissance. But his *Orbecche* gained distinction in more than one way. It was staged in 1541 at the court of Ferrara, where theatrical productions had been held in high esteem for nearly half a century. Befitting a man of the Renaissance, he was quick in laying claim to "fame perpetual" that his *Orbecche* should go down in history as the first Italian tragedy introduced into the theater. Whatever music the performance of the *Orbecche* needed was composed by Alfonso della Viola.

Although the features of his tragedies were distinctly marked, they lacked the graces of attractiveness and even originality. With thought impoverished and artistic vision blinded, Giraldi, like others before and after, understood the tragic to manifest itself only by the record of criminal action, and he had nothing else to show but ghastly atrocities, crime piled upon crime, lusty murders so ferocious that even the gods turned their heads away from the gruesome sight. In violation of the Greek rule that the savage deeds must never be shown, Giraldi had them at times committed on the stage for all to see. The complete misconception of the tragic, impelling as it did an accursed propensity to unsavory cruelties, unfortunately formed a school of Italian dramatists who apparently tried to undo each other's zeal in being ever more tragic, that is, ever more savage. Hence it could happen, and it did in fact, that *Mors acerba*, bitter death, the reaper, played such havoc among the dramatis personae that at the end of the play none but the minor characters of the cast had escaped the wholesale slaughter.

All the Italian tragedies of the Renaissance suffered from the defect which ensued from the erroneous conceit of the tragic. Now, does it stand to reason that an error of judgment must lead to artistic failure? Is it not rather inability for the poetic expression of the tragic in dramatic form that was the root of all deficiency? Alessandro Tassoni shortly after 1600 looked back upon the dramatic achievements of the Renaissance and, sure of the power of his judgment, asserted that not a single author of a tragedy had yet surpassed the measure of mediocrity. Uncertain of the reasons, he suggested that perhaps the poets lacked good fortune on their side, or perhaps the Italian language might be capable of expressing the serious and momentous only in imperfect ways. These reasons cannot satisfy the quest. If good fortune lacked, it could be nothing else but the good fortune of rejoicing in the possession of a great poet. The Trissinos, Giraldis, Speronis, verify that Fortuna did not smile upon the Italian tragedians; and she did not change her moods in times to come.

It has often been observed by the most competent connoisseurs that the Italian dramatists never accomplished great tragedies. In the eighteenth century Vittorio Alfieri started a flicker of hope only soon to be dashed. Of all the reasons marshaled by Italian writers to explain the failure, the responsibility cast upon opera demands our attention, if only for a moment. The "exaggerated pleasure which all the world takes from the music drama" appeared to Maffei as the real culprit that prevented the tragedy from coming into its own as a drama. And Alfieri, more outspoken still, in a rage named opera "the most tasteless and dullest entertainment of the whole of Italy." When he entered upon writing his tragedies, he furiously declared that his drama would be composed of a verse which under no condition would yield to being sung. But is a verse unmusical a verse?

That opera should have debarred the Italian dramatist from achieving great tragedy out of his own poetic resources is meaningless, if not absurd. It is precisely as absurd as if we were to say that the presence of great tragedies such as those of Shakespeare thwarted the endeavor of the English to accomplish a great opera of their own. And what of the Italian tragedies before opera existed, the tragedies of the Renaissance which, if actually staged, included some strains of solo song and the music of the chorus, but were never composed in full? No matter what the crave for opera, music had not been an impediment on the road of the tragedian as opera and tragedy do not exclude each other. It may well be that for shaping the tragic the musician possessed what the dramatist lacked: genius.

Now, is the story of "music drama reborn" really nothing but a story which records the miscarriage of the tragedy? And are the dramatic works we talked about within the range of the theme at all? In a sense usually attributed to the opera or even to the dramatic music of the years around 1600, they are not. This sense, however, does not embrace all that entered into the scope of the renascent music drama. We have been told time after time that music had been no more than incidental, hence irrelevant to the tragedies or other dramas of the Renaissance; never in touch with the substance of a music drama proper, it did not fashion the mind of the musician as a dramatist.

It is true that the composer selected, or was advised to choose, merely certain sections of the text, parts of the monologue and always the chorus, although the chorus all too often expatiated on action and events, and if in a contemplative mood did not reach the loftiness of choral lyrics. The curtailment of the musician's work did not result from deficiencies of a fundamental concept or from an inability to venture for the cause of the full gain. The musician held back from engaging his creative powers to forge the whole tragedy into artistic shape because the demand for confining the diffusion of music within narrow bounds had its support in the theory of the humanists. If the Italian tragedy was driven to vie with its ancient model, it had to comply with some of the conditions which were thought to have determined the model. Although all humanists agreed that the chorus of the tragedy must always be sung, they were at variance when they came to decide upon the share of music in the monologue. Which parts were sung and which omitted? Questions such as these were argued about as though they were not problems of scholarship but tenets of faith, with the proponents of opposing views all bursting into the language of passion. And most of the humanists were rightly convinced that not all of Greek tragedy had been subject to musical composition.

If the drama of the Renaissance conceded to music but a limited place, it fell in with the requirements of the school of thought which denied music the right of controlling the drama as a whole. When the *Oedipus Rex* of Sophocles, regarded by many a man of many an age as the greatest of all tragedies, was to be staged at the opening of the celebrated Teatro Olimpico in Vicenza, an architectural marvel, no lesser a musician than Andrea Gabrieli had been charged to lend his genius to the composition needed, but only for the chorus of the tragedy, because no other part was thought to admit of any music. We do not dare deny the extraordinary work its rightful place of prominence in the history of music drama reborn.

But the school of thought which held that music was appointed to fulfill no more than a partial task within the drama lost ground when the sixteenth century came to its close. Francesco Patrici, hardly ever mentioned and yet for his time amazingly informed about Greek poetry and poets, made valuable comments on Greek tragedy when he talked about melody in his learned treatise *Della Poetica*, a history, as it were, of Greek poetry and music which appeared in 1586. And there he recorded his view: "che tutta la Tragedia, che di attori era composta, e di choro si cantava"; that the whole tragedy, composed of actors and the chorus, was sung. And this, precisely, was the belief which gave birth to the music drama set to music from start to finish, the music drama which we are wont to attribute to the research and discussions advanced by Giovanni Bardi with the assistance of men such as Vincenzo Galilei, Girolamo Mei, Corsi, Peri, Caccini, and others, in the Platonic academy of Florence, known as the Camerata Fiorentina.

Francesco Patrici demands our attention in another respect, even if only at the margin of the matter at hand. We all are aware of the fervent spirit which the Florentines brought to bear upon their deep concern with all the aspects of Greek music. In the wake of their enthusiastic studies Vincenzo Galilei published a document on Greek music for the first time in history. We always believed that the Greek notation of music remained a closed book of mystery to all the Florentines. Now, Francesco Patrici analyzed a fragment of Galilei's document with the assistance of that theoretical source which holds the key to the riddle of the

Greek notation: the famous tables of Alypius. Though not a member of the Camerata, Patrici conversed on the matter with Giovanni Bardi, and they came to agree on the interpretation. They are likely to have talked about other aspects of Greek poetry and music as well; with their like interests and combined efforts they may have seen eye to eye with one another when it came to define the music of the drama. And Francesco Patrici, Giovanni Bardi, and Girolamo Mei all were acquainted with the noble attainments of the humanist Piero Vettori, the editor of Greek tragedies and commentator of Aristotle's *Poetics*.

When called upon to re-create the ancient tragedy by having music hold its undivided reign over the drama in its entirety, the Florentine musicians must have reared their progeny in faithful obedience to the principle, esteemed to be authentically Greek, that all the elements, the monologue and dialogue as well as the chorus, should go into the musical cast. At this juncture of circumstances it is, neither to the scholar nor to anyone else, of the slightest importance whether the assumed principle concurred with the realities of history or the deceits of a phantom. For only by translating the concept literally into the terms of actual art did the modern music drama, the opera, come to be set upon its irresistible course.

Whatever else the Florentine musicians boasted of having worked out for the cause of restoring music to its ancient dignity—the monody as a solo song, or the *stile recitativo* as the main medium of the dramatic monologue, or the revision of the intercourse between word and tone—was by no means as sensationally new without a precedent as they would have liked their contemporaries to believe; and it did not match the importance of having completely translated a dramatic text into the language of music. All merits, or should we rather say, the only claim to the merit of perpetuity that can be conferred upon the Florentine musicians, must be traced to the allotted task of having supplied a complete translation.

If we appraise the artistic value, even within the brief span of the epoch itself and apart from measuring the dramatic adequacy of the musical expression, works such as the *Euridice* of Giulio Caccini or Jacopo Peri forfeit their worth no matter where we look for the just gauge of our judgment. Regardless of what has been said to the glory of the Florentines either by the members of the Camerata Fiorentina or by historians of music, no effort of ours can raise the price of their compositions. The Italian tragedians of the past were extolled—or extolled themselves—for having brought about the *tragoedia rediviva,* though by accomplishment they never surpassed the average for want of true genius. In the same manner the Florentine musicians failed as composers, and they failed for the same reason. But while among the dramatists great talent did not appear, the music drama met its genius—Claudio Monteverdi.

If the new music drama owed its birth to the observance of a rule which was thought to have been established by ancient tragedians, it is no more than legitimate to ask if the music drama reborn was a tragedy in its own right. It must be said at the outset that the new music drama did not clarify the tragedy as a special category of dramatic art. The names chosen by the composers independently or in harmony with the poets vary from work to work; *favola in musica, favola pastorale, dramma per musica, dramma musicale, opera rappresentata in musica,* are the designations most frequently used. Titles such as *tragedia* or *tragedia musicale* are rare exceptions; now and then we come across a *tragicomedia*.

Rinuccini's *Euridice* begins with a prologue sung by Tragedia herself, the tragic muse, entrusted by her very nature with the song of grievous and lamentable scenes. But now she will change, and change she must, lest her voice jar the felicitous occasion. She casts off the mournful buskin and gloomy attire to waken more gentle affections:

> ecco i mesti coturni e i foschi panni
> cangio, e desto ne i cor più dolci affetti.

But the poet hardly would have called the tragic muse upon the scene had he not thought that the fate of Eurydice belonged to tragedy, however mellowed by the *fin lieto*, the happy ending.

And the *Arianna* of Rinuccini, composed by Monteverdi, is expressly called a *tragedia*. Abandoned by Theseus, a victim of the conflict between love and honor, Ariadne rises to be a tragic figure; but in fulfillment of the myth the *fin lieto* brings about her marriage with the god Dionysus. If the divine union no longer bears the tragic mask, it brings the old alliance with the Bacchic cult to life.

One more work, also called a tragedy, deserves being mentioned: the *Adone* of Vendramin. It was presumably but not certainly composed by Monteverdi; at all events, the music is lost. As the epic poem of Giambattista Marino had been the source of inspiration, the ancient story of Venus and Adonis vested but one thing in the tragic, the affluence of human passion.

Among the music dramas, then, there are but few tragedies so named, to say nothing of the works which despite their title go without the inner characteristics of a tragedy.

In the light of the frequency of the themes chosen from ancient tragedies for operatic composition—the *Didone, Giasone, Egisto, Ipermestra, Eteocle e Polinice,* and many another—let there be no mistake that the tragic theme impelled the librettist to fasten on the course of tragedy. More often than not, he parried the fateful blows by the *lieto fine.*

Although the music drama reborn did not become a *tragoedia rediviva,* it did resound of the tragic, but in its own and particular way. If among the music dramas we seek a tragedy that is the integral and unblemished representative of its kind, we shall seek in vain. For the music drama, whether called a tragedy or not, drifted away from the tragedy as an impeccable work of art to the tragic as a human condition, and perhaps the change came to drift with the tide of the drama of Euripides.

When Aristophanes, with the sharp tongue of irony, portrayed the dispute between Euripides and Aeschylus, with the god Dionysus sitting in as the arbiter, the younger dramatist bore the brunt of the reproach that he had introduced the theme of human passion, of love confounded and confounding, and thereby spoiled the noble tragedy of old.

And love, the rulership of Amor, emerging, in every disguise of the ancient myth, story, or legend, as the main, if not exclusive, theme of the new music drama came to be the condition of the tragic. Human passions unbridled and ambitions unbound surging to their peak caused suffering, violence, and conflicts which when resolved showed the tragic to be a momentary constellation, and not of lasting continuance.

The potential of the tragic for the musician, therefore, had its roots in human nature and in the reality of life rather than in Fate or in a propitious shape of the artistic drama,

57

and, consequently, the dramatic text did not need the artistic unity of an accomplished tragedy or a perfection all its own.

This must have been Monteverdi's thought when he insisted that human passions must always be the subject of dramatic texts, when he insisted on suffering and conflicts such as those of *Orfeo* or *Arianna*. For it is he who, by his vision, makes his thrust into the depth of human nature and uncovers the tragedy of human passions. Such is the fabric of his human drama, and it is the fabric of music drama reborn.

IV

Tragedy and the Music Drama

"Men must know, that in this theatre of man's life it is reserved only for God and angels to be lookers on." Perhaps there is no better preamble to the music drama, to the opera of the baroque age, than this motto expressed by Francis Bacon in his *Advancement of Learning*. For the theater is the mirror of life, and life is but a theatrical spectacle. Not that man of the baroque age was first in speaking of life as a "spectaculum mundi," as a theater of the world. But he seized upon the ancient metaphor to impress it with the seal of his own mind. Calderón cast the *Gran Teatro del Mundo* into a play where the King, the Rich, the Wise, Beauty, the Farmer, and the Beggar were appointed to act their parts on the stage of life before God, Lord and final judge of the performance they had given during their brief span of earthly existence. "Be mindful," the Spanish poet Francisco Gómez de Quevedo uttered, "that life is a spectacle and this whole world the great stage where the scenes change in a trice and all of us play as the actors with God being the sole dramaturgist."

This very concept of the world as a theater, seen by Calderón with his inward eye to the divine order of all things and events, attained, in the epoch of the baroque, the highest degree of an artistic manifestation brimful of pathos. And within the world of the baroque theater, it was the music drama, the opera, which brought about the magic fulfillment of this concept.

In the opera, there is but one who has the rightful claim to having his life mirrored on the stage: a man of high station towering above the common lot from the lofty tiers of the human hierarchy, kings and princes, the "personaggi grandi," the world's commanders. That only men of wondrous distinction were allowed to be spoken of in the drama was no doubt the sequel to the ancient intelligence that tragedy never dealt with anything but the fate and actions of the great. The prince of the baroque age, who thought himself enthroned by divine right, saw his own station glorified in the opera, a tribute to his being by an artistic enhancement. With whatever names the heroes of history or mythology echoed the greatness of the past tragedy, they were but spokesmen of the present in disguise. Divinities became mere agents of the glorification of ruling masters who did not seek an enigmatic symbol of their power, but first and last their own identity. Wherever the symbolism seemed to be suggestive of the past, it was the reality of the present that prevailed.

The heroes of Greek tragedy though of royal descent were always so contrived as to abide by the true measure of the human race; or, as Aristotle gleaned from the dramas he knew, they might be slightly better than what nature ordinarily provided, but they must never exceed human proportions. The heroes of the baroque opera, however, departed from these measures, and their conduct wore a different complexion. The reaches of their aspirations were pushed beyond the limits of the realm of nature; nature held a frame to be broken through and surpassed. For the sake of transcending nature and with a firm trust that Fortuna befriends only the strong and the bold, "Fortes fortuna adiuvat," the heroes of the opera appeared unremittingly tuned to the high pitch of exaggeration.

Because the libretti never ceased telling the story of an oversized heroism, they aroused a feeling of annoyance, especially toward the end of the baroque age when the relationship to nature and the natural conduct of man came up for a critical review. And modern criticism has scarcely ever lowered its voice when judging the libretti of the baroque *dramma musicale regio e politico* as plays. Even looked upon as literature, however, they are better than their reputation. The production of an opera as a play apart from its music rarely occurred; the performance of Cicognini's *Giasone* without the music of Cavalli is the exception that proves the rule.

Designed from the outset to be furnished with music, the baroque libretti generally represent a category of drama all its own; they must be judged with the view to the vast range of all their elements. All the elements dwell together in a unity within which the perfection of one might compensate for the flaw of another. But it is only the confluence of all, mingling their concerted action, which made the baroque opera a spectacle of the world the like of which had not been seen before. The grandiloquence of the heroes, the majestic style of the musical pathos, and the dazzling splendor and pompous pageantry on the stage are all descendants of one and the same spirit, and if we find fault with one of the descendants, we must find fault with all.

As an art work the baroque opera was deliberately set at constant strife with nature, for the conceit of conquering nature determined the artistic enterprise, and conquering nature meant surpassing it. All the straining and stretching of the components to extremes issued from the aspiration for achieving art by outdoing nature or anything else that the artist might have taken as the basis from which to start. If historical figures were chosen to play their role in the opera, they usually were distorted past recognition; if mythology was drawn upon, the divinities were promptly identified with the human heroes of the opera; and if fairy tales provided the material, they stood in favor because they themselves had the capacity for exaggeration, the miraculous, the excess over and above reality, the happy ending. Decorative elements, in the past confined to their subsidiary function, claimed to be the essential propriety, rather than an accidental ornament. Thus, the constituents subject to the melodic ornamentation of the sixteenth century now were given the firmness and function of melodic substance—this was the basis for the soloistic *stile concertante*—and whatever decorative expression musicians coveted burst forth from the ornate basis of the style with the exuberance of extravagant coloraturas testifying that art must outdo nature.

But the theatrical art of the baroque opera did not rest only on a metamorphosis of the accidental into the essential, not only on stress and overstress, nor on powerful gradations alone. The world of appearance mirrored on the stage exerted its inescapable charm for all the illusion that it granted. The *haut monde* of kings and princes, palaces of large extent and glorious architecture, heavenly and terrestrial abodes of gods and heroes, views of exotic and fairy lands far distant or never seen but with the eye of fancy, large crowds attendant to the *personaggi grandi*, sham battles on sea and on land, visions into the vast and the above, a rapid and frequent change of scenes—all these orgies of spectacle, feasting human senses on the world's beauty of appearance, deceitfully engaged an unresolved play of the real against the unreal, with the arts of illusory scenography triumphant. Yet a tragic conflict pierced all these illusions of the baroque theater. The spectacle, with all its enticement, seemed to sound like a perpetual appeal *Memento vivere* (Be mindful of life), but the echo that came back from behind the glittering façade steadfastly voiced a *Memento mori* (Be mindful of death).

And this internal conflict between reality and the world beyond the world of appearance acted upon the very core of the opera, despite the inordinate sensuality which hardly ever receded from the foreground of the scene even though the voice from the prompter's box tried to preach the sermon of virtue. The theme that governed all, and might have governed life as well as the theater, had been invariably love, Amor, whose arrows hurt, but also soothe the inflicted pains with the balm of hope for ultimate satisfaction. Glory without which life is not worth living, love that is teeming with intricate deceits, *costanza e fortezza*, constancy and fortitude—not always an impenetrable armor against the violent assaults of love—honor and nobility, magnanimity and baseness, feigned innocence and disguised depravity, all flowed together to unleash the "commozion d'affetti," the whirlwind of affections.

The code of noble station required that all passions, emotions, or feelings must have the stately measure of intensity becoming *personaggi grandi*, and the artistic principles of the baroque further increased the intensity by the nature of its style. In a manner characteristic of the baroque opera, dramatists and musicians alike repeatedly spoke of the "forza delle passioni," the force of passions, as being the fiber of great men and their proper style. For "le style est l'homme même," style is the man himself, and this is manifest in life and in art. The old demand "Si vis me flere, plorandum est," which Horace included in his *Ars Poetica*, the demand that we must adequately lament if we really wish the listener to cry, acquired new significance in that nothing but extreme force, the utmost of passionate expression, seemed to be adequate for a convincing presentation. This casts full light upon the reason for the grandeur of passions in the baroque opera. The scenes built upon passions violently expressed carried even their own name; they were called "scene di forza," and it was understood that such scenes of force must make their regular and frequent appearance in every opera.

Passions, however, should always be varied and by their variety they necessarily opposed each other. For this alone granted the conflict between them all, the "commozion d'affetti," which became the essence of dramatic opera. But the mover of all the intrigues and struggles, of the stratagems, the "inganni," which drove men to their violent actions would always be the god Amor; for "l'amorosa passione de tutte le altre trionfi[a]," the passion of love triumphed over all other emotions. And there was nothing Platonic about this love although the hero of the opera might ecstatically sing of his conviction that while his eyes feasted on the beauty of the body, they searched only after the "bell' anima," the beautiful soul, of the beloved.

"Amore e guerra," love and war—this motto of synonyms, engraved upon every baroque opera, lay at the roots of all dramatic action and of all tragic conflicts. Though conflicts pretend to play secretly upon the human soul, to tear the very intestines of man, they were in fact exhibited by the baroque urge of demonstrative display. "Fan con l'armi un aspra guerra/ Nel mio sen sdegno e l'amore" (Wrath and Love fight with their arms a bitter war in my bosom), sings Adalberto in Antonio Sartorio's opera *L'Adelaide* (1672), and he sings as if he were the herald of a public message rather than the keeper of a painful secret. War and love, Amor and Mars, persistently occupied the stage ever since the voluptuous verse of Marino had told the story of Venus and Adonis, and ever since Claudio Monteverdi made the madrigals amorous and warlike, "amorosi e guerrieri," the theme of dramatic composition, the promoter of tragic conflicts. The war between human passions, "la guerra delle passioni," gave the marks of tragedy or of the tragic to the baroque opera, and in describing it we cannot surpass the verse of Meredith:

> In tragic life, God wot,
> No villain need be! Passions spin the plot.

When passions were pitted against each other ready to clash with all the force of charged emotions, and when desires collided with obstacles and rivals, the battle of contending ambitions carried the dramatic theme to its own nature as well as to its tragic issues, and like any bellicose action it left combatants wounded or dead, losers and victors.

The *stile concertante*, the musical style which grew with the baroque music drama and even placed its signature upon the shape of the drama itself, which furnished, as it were, the arms for the fray of passions, was fraught with the meaning of fight, contention, and competition between the musical elements and characteristics of composition. Now, we are told with untiring persistence that the word "concerto," "concertante," must not be derived from "concertare," to fight, to vie with one another, but must be seen in the light of "concentus," of that which sounds together. This explanation had been laid down as law by the Crusca, the Academy which held the guardianship over the Italian, that is, Tuscan, language. Although we shall not be so frivolous as to rebut the authority of an academy, Italian or otherwise, we shall maintain with equally untiring persistence that in the baroque age there was a school of thought which firmly believed in the *stile concertante* to mean "concertare," to fight; and the rhetoric of the time, familiar with the term "concertatio," combat, strongly supported the interpretation. It was by no means uncommon to speak with reference to the style of "certamina musica," musical contests, of the "bellum musicale," the musical war. And when the baroque musician talked about the *stile concertante*, he did not concern himself with the etymology of the word, as he had no designs on being *Il Cruscante Impazzito*, The Maddened Academician of the Crusca, who had been honored by an amusing "Tragicomedia" with music interspersed and written by either Benedetto Marcello or a Francesco Aricci. And many a composer can be called to the witness stand to testify that the competitive element, this ever active principle which is a drama of artistic energies by itself, comes within the essence of the *stile concertante*.

The sense of elements in contest imparted to the *stile concertante* a virtue propitious to dramatic music. It would be even more correct to say that the theme of the baroque opera, the tempest of passions, gave the style its ability to render passions in strife. If music becomes an illustration of man, of tragic life, as it did when Monteverdi gave musical composition a new purpose, it reveals both the temper of human emotion and the play of passions upon each other with the artist's mind delving into the deep pit of human nature. When at the beginning of his dramatic work Monteverdi sounded out the human tragedy of Ariadne, he admitted that he had none to instruct him and no musical guide to lead him through the secrets of expressing human passions in music, save Plato's doctrine of imitation. And when late in his life, close to the time of the *Incoronazione di Poppea*, he wrote that he was engrossed in the philosophic research of natural science, he confessed that this inquiry into the nature of man served him better than any professional guidance, and what he harvested from these studies went, as he said, into his artistic work. None had been greater than Monteverdi in bringing to the fore the conflict of demonic passions, profound melancholy, and tragic suffering. Dio of Prusa said that the artist must be none other than the *mimetes tes daimonias physeos*, the imitator of the demonic nature. This precisely concurs with what Monteverdi regarded as the business of the artist.

For the sake of the *ariosi spectacoli*, a term which ambiguously wavers between "airy" spectacles and spectacles of "arias," the composers, beginning with Monteverdi himself, strained all their efforts to build up musical rhetoric expressive of passions, and carried the *stile concertante*, the style of competitive implements, to its widest range and to perfection. Now, the arias of passionate emotions—of jealousy, wrath, ire, warlike fortitude, of all the multifarious beguilements of love, of the lament over the tragic loss, over misery and pain, suffering and death—were all subject to the standards of style, with the structure and figurative materials establishing the scope of expression. And when the arias followed each other, driven by Amor, the mover of action, they came in succession as image followed image, truly *ariosi spectacoli*, and the whole was nothing less than a war of antagonistic forces, with the *stile concertante* being the most faithful interpreter of conflicting passions. But only an art which marshaled all the refined idioms of musical rhetoric into the rigor of a ceremonious style was capable of rising above the ambiguities of emotional expression. Indeed, the composer relied so completely on the perfect mechanism of the stylish vocabulary that he needed no extraneous indication of the passion he wished to reveal, though on occasion he took recourse to a special instruction to designate the shades he fancied. An unequivocal rhetoric strengthened his steadfast belief in the powers of music to demonstrate human passions in terms at once effective and infallible.

In accordance with all artistic elements being under the stern rule of a monumental style, the manner of performance contributed its share to the demonstration of conflicting passions by gesture and the mode of singing. Visitors to Italy who attended the presentation of operas marveled not only at the splendor of display and the grandeur of the music, but also at the conduct and manner of the singers. As the passions themselves had the force and stateliness befitting great personalities, the style demanded that expression match their measure; and in expressing violent emotions, violence was precisely what the word implies. Emphatic presentation sounded as though it were a permanent exaggeration. Anger became storming rage, sorrow called for the wails of pain, anxiety appeared as tragic agony, and all this was shown not only by the demonstrative gesture—as the Italian singers were praised for being perfect actors—but also in the emphatic manner of singing. The voices were hard, forceful, loud, and impetuous, even harsh to the ears of some of the foreign listeners. At all events, they lacked the sweet charms of sentimentality, as great passions do not suffer from the softness of mediocre feelings. Fascination with the voices of the *castrati*, to whom all the heroic parts of the opera from Monteverdi's *Orfeo* on were assigned, evinced the artificial characteristics of a style which in vying with nature asserted the superiority of art by bold digressions from the natural size of things.

What then was tragedy in the Italian music drama of the baroque? Is it such a conflict as Monteverdi rendered in his *Incoronazione di Poppea?* The betrayal of Ottone by Poppea; the divorce of Nerone from Ottavia, the empress; the conspiracy of murdering Poppea; the ruthless removal of all hindrances that stood in the way of ardent ambitions, even to the extent of killing Seneca, the imperial counselor of moderation, wisdom, and restraint; the banishment of Ottavia from Rome and Roman lands—all this converged in encounters with the impact on the tragic. But the final triumph of love-ridden Nerone and Poppea, burnt by the fire of ambition for glory and fame, seems to oust the drama from the realm of tragedy. Is that which a moral judgment would brand with the stigma of triumphant vice the happy ending which turned a tragedy into a tragicomedy? However much our moral conscience might revolt, the measure of judging the principles of baroque opera would be more appropriately taken in accordance with the verse from Milton's *Paradise Lost:*

> To reign is worth ambition though in hell:
> Better to reign in hell, than serve in heav'n.

Whether or not we regard as a happy resolution an outcome which attained the ultimate satisfaction of amorous and ambitious passions at all cost and by any unscrupulous device, the *fin lieto* did not dull the sharp edges of the weapon which in the course of the drama had done its work of tragic injuries; it did not heal all the wounds which offense, intrigues, and thwarted desires inflicted while passions were in battle, to say nothing of those whom death slayed with the mortal blow. When all is over and the *fin lieto* reached, it is—significantly enough—the poignant music of the forceful scenes that we retain.

Yet not always did the melodrama of the Italian baroque arrive at a happy ending. To be sure, more often than not the story of Rinaldo and Armida was deprived of the tragic outcome which Tasso had immortalized, and the tragedy of Dido abandoned departed from the course designed by Virgil. Metastasio restored the tragic catastrophe of Dido, although his heroes began to sing with the graces of a softer age. It seems, however, to be remarkable that the Italian opera, at least of the seventeenth century, preserved the calamities of tragedy, murder, the finality of death, wherever Seneca's tragedy still wielded its influence upon the opera, that is, whenever the theme dealt with the story of a tyrant. Pompeo must die because he obstructed despotic power, and Caesar met with death because he was thought to be a tyrant. Antonino was killed in Sartorio's opera because of his tyrannic rulership. Sejano, in that remarkable double opera *Prosperity and Fall of Elio Sejano,* by Antonio Sartorio (1667), came to his awful end because he usurped tyranny. His last curse when committing suicide in prison— that with his downfall Rome, the whole universe, be plunged over the precipice of chaos—echoed the very words of Atreus in Seneca's *Thyestes.*

Apart from these relics of Latin drama, the opera hardly

ever let death occur as the inescapable sequel of guilt and fateful entanglement, hardly ever allowed catastrophe to be the climactic conclusion of the tragedy. Even if death occurred in the course of the music drama, it often was but an incidental crime, perpetrated either in rage, the passionate outburst of a moment, or for the sake of punishing the villain, or even by an error because of mistaken identities. We gladly record, however, that compared with the tragedies of the sixteenth century the rate of mortality had considerably decreased in the heroic opera of the baroque. Sanguinary excesses no longer were proof of the presence of tragedy.

But the plots of crimes were all the more frequent in the imbroglio of intrigues at cross purposes to each other. Vengeance, jealousy, offended honor, or assailed virtue lured the plotters into wily conspiracies to bring about the ruin of the opponent. If the plot miscarried, it did so not because of its being badly contrived, but because of the interference of a superior plotter, Amor, the exalted intriguer whose whims were command and settled all the discords. The intervention of the divine force had nothing abstract about it, for the divinities had the habit of appearing in the flesh. When the sword was drawn, the dagger pointed to perform the dreadful deed, the god Amor intercepted execution in the nick of time. Though such an appearance tallied with the baroque hankering after display, the visible, the *demonstratio ad oculos*, it does not fully satisfy if we must understand it as an intervention of Fate. And here we are face to face with the essential problem of Fate in the tragic opera of the baroque.

What is the baroque Fate and where is its realm? Is it in

heaven; is Fate the Christian Providence? Is it in Olympus where pagan gods reside; is Fate the Moira of the ancient tragedy? Is it a supreme force, beyond the clouds of earth and life, which, though invisible and undefinable, forever holds its hand over man and all his vagrancies? In the prologues of the operas, divinities or divine forces personified pretend to forge the destiny of the heroes whose life and actions are about to be unfolded. And gods and goddesses are ready to appear at any time, although now and then only to symbolize the godlike prowess of man—as in Sartorio's opera when Antonino, the vicious tyrant and vile huntsman, on his amorous chase of love came down on the wings of an eagle, just as Zeus used tricky disguises whenever he impregnated every beautiful woman he could discover. But gods who intervene or make their appearance in the opera are not really the makers, not even the messengers, of Fate. And yet, the heroes, in spite or because of all their apparel of style, seem to be driven by a force which, acting inside themselves but in semblance from the outside, was stronger than man. In other words, passions that govern the baroque heroes of Italian opera ravage the human soul like demons; and it is precisely the demonic nature of human passions that made action appear as though it were guided by a fateful force. This does not imply that all passions must be necessarily evil even if they have their demonic grip over human souls. It merely means that man possessed by passion proceeds entirely in accordance with its commands without any real freedom of action. If anything played the role of Fate in the baroque opera it was not Providence, not Moira, but man himself under the sway of the demon of his passion.

This would seem to be the most propitious ground for a

tragedy to grow its fruits at their best. But the taste of the time, which dreaded the course of irrevocable catastrophe and, in its stead, yearned for the happy ending, spoiled the favorable conditions and admitted no more than tragic situations, not a tragedy. The librettist, barred from the boldness of genius, readily complied with the digressions of fashion. The Italian music drama of the baroque is not an unbroken tragedy, but a diverse drama with tragic episodes protruding and the happy ending prevalent.

If we attempt to balance the weight of the tragic components against the Aristotelian definition, does the music drama show compassion, terror, and the final catharsis to be in the scales? Can we expect the mere display of passions to effect the tragic catharsis? Is it not that only the inescapable catastrophe accords cathartic bliss? Now, the passions, spurred—it is true—by the pathos of the baroque style and yet deep-seated in the temperament of human nature, were the tragic cause of misery and suffering. And the hero, the blind tool of his demonic disposition and the suffering victim of his own passion, had the rightful claim to compassion of those who listened to his loud voice of anguish, ire, pride, or wantonness. The violent conflict of stormy passions, the savage struggle between adverse emotions where greater power seems to be the only recognized rule of the contest, might be looked upon with compassion, if not pity. But cathartic terror, that fear aroused when Fate is seen to drive the hero to the abyss of catastrophe, could hardly ever come from the tragic, or merely violent, accidents in the music drama. We take our compassion as a guide in the labyrinth of passions, and if we are unwilling to concede that insight into the mysteries of the passionate nature of man matches the Aristotelian catharsis, we nevertheless must admit that the spontaneous revelation of human nature conveys a blissfulness at least congenial to the awful intelligence of tragedy.

When we speak of revelation, or of tragic compassion aroused, we speak of music and musician alone, of the composer whose art draws the curtain from the complexities of human nature. For it is always the musician, never the librettist, who expresses the "agonizanti accenti," the agonizing accents. When in the opera *Egisto* Climene sings her melancholy lament "Piangete occhi dolenti," it is not the text but the pungent melody of Cavalli that reveals the affection of grief. Were it not for the impetuous *stile concertante* which Sartorio ingeniously shaped in his *Adelaide*, we would not be able to imagine the emotional upheaval of the heroine. And when Griselda, offended by the odious demands of Ottone, is faced with the choice between the sacrifice of her virtue and the death of her son, her words are but a theatrical exclamation, shallow and ridiculous: "Figlio! Tiranno! oh Dio! che far poss' io"; Son, Tyrant, oh Lord! What can I do? Yet Alessandro Scarlatti translated her agony of mind into one of the most forceful scenes presenting the conflict of emotions. And what would Cleopatra's tragic aria "Se pietà di me non senti" be without the music of Handel? It is the musician, and surely the great one alone, who, by sounding out the profundity of passion with the measure of his vision into the depth of human nature, turns an ordinarily dim feeling into the limpid manifestation of an august style.

The capacity of the musician, rather than the skills of the dramatist, will be convincing in the end. Nothing proves more strikingly the truth of the matter than a comparison between the Italian baroque opera and the French *tragédie lyrique* of Jean-Baptiste Lully. All tragedies of Quinault, the librettist of Lully, are by far superior to any seventeenth-century Italian libretto because Corneille and Racine shaped, however slightly, the artistic mind of the French librettist. And none of the *tragédies lyriques*, uniform, though not wholly in keeping with the drama of the great French tragedians, could ever stand the test of being compared with the opera of Cavalli, Sartorio, or Legrenzi, to say nothing of Monteverdi. This judgment is by no means pitched to the disputes of the time whether the French or Italian concept of music had the claim to superiority. Nothing can slight the genius of Lully, an Italian, who miraculously translated the nature of the French language into musical terms. No criticism will rob his *tragédie lyrique* of its consistency in dramatic procedure. And in stateliness he probably did not have an equal. Even if we disregard the heavy political burden which Lully placed upon his work by making the *tragédie en musique* the "témoin de la gloire immortelle D'un roi l'étonnement des Rois. Et des plus grands Héros le plus parfait modèle," the witness of the immortal glory of a king, the marvel of kings, and among the greatest heroes the most perfect model—a political tendency which surely added a special grandeur of style to the French opera—Lully's tragedy even at its best, and his *Armide* is no doubt among the best French operas, has not the power of conviction which animated the dramatic music of Cavalli or Sartorio, simply because musical genius did not abound with him. And again, greater musical genius strikes the balance in favor not of Lully, but of Rameau's *tragédie lyrique*.

It is characteristic that the artistic influence of the French opera, wherever it made itself felt, led to a remarkable concentration of drama, to an improvement of the libretto, to a more consistent, if not deeper, grasp of tragedy. This is proved by Tommaso Traëtta—often misunderstood and unfairly overshadowed by the figure of Gluck—in the splendid style and display of his *Sofonisba*, and in his *Antigona* as well, despite its disgraceful departure from the tragic close.

The reform opera of Gluck also owes much of its substance to the *tragédie lyrique* and the French concept of drama. Actually, without the French tradition, even the Italian versions of *Orfeo* and *Alceste* would never have arisen in the shape of the tragedies which Gluck rendered in the later part of his life. Yet we are always aware of the calculating mind that brought about the reform of opera, or—as it has been called—the revolution in dramatic music.

Persuaded by a propitious constellation Gluck—like others before him and around him—reacted critically to the frills and foam of Italian opera. "When I undertook to compose the opera *Alceste*," he declared, "I designed stripping it wholly of all the abuses which, introduced either by the ill-contrived vanity of the singers or by the all-too great forbearance of the composers, for a long time disfigured the Italian opera and made of the stateliest and the most beautiful of all spectacles the most ridiculous and the most annoying."

And from behind this reaction to "abuses" came the drive to unleash style and nature from their fetters. All the abuses were "style" and all that truthfulness of expression needed was the simplicity of nature. Passions are truthfully expressed if they are naturally voiced. But any composer of the baroque would have maintained that the style of his expression most fittingly suited the nature of passion; and

Gluck's own work proves that style cannot be dislodged by crying out for nature.

Burney, the astute connoisseur of baroque opera, an inveterate admirer of Hasse, said that "Gluck's genius seems more calculated for exciting terror in painting difficult situations, occasioned by complicated misery, and the tempestuous fury of unbridled passions." And true it is that despite the reform, human passions are still the theme which contrives the tragedies of Gluck. If his highly rationalistic opera unfastened the forces of reform or revolution, the revolution did not outlive his day; nor did it reach far beyond his own work. Rarely was there a revolution that had so little repercussion. Not even Mozart, the most visionary listener of the time, quickest of hearing, perceived any repercussion of a revolution, though he was not insensitive to the style of Gluck. In spite of his *Idomeneo* he put no faith in any aspect of Gluck's reform. And when Mozart himself soared to the height of his dramatic work, he reached the peak on a path of his own without the designs of a "reformer."

Schiller once wrote a letter to Goethe—it was at the end of 1797—where he said that he always kept a certain confidence in the opera, a hope that opera might shed, like the dithyrambic choruses of the old Bacchic festivals, a tragedy of nobler shape; for by the power of music opera could grant pathos a freer play and admit indulgently even the marvelous, so that we would be more indifferent to the material, the theme, the topic. Goethe promptly, on the following day, answered that Schiller would have seen his hopes largely fulfilled if he had heard *Don Giovanni*. But this work, Goethe added, is totally isolated, and Mozart's death shattered all prospects of something like it. Is Mozart's

Don Giovanni the drama that arose from the deep shafts of music to the surface as Greek tragedy arose out of the Dionysian dithyramb? Can an opera that was marked "Dramma giocoso" betoken the features of tragedy?

Not swayed by the fruitless discussions on the number of serious and comical parts in *Don Giovanni*, and unwilling to concede to the recording historian the final verdict in the matter, I venture to say that Goethe was closer to the truth than many a master of professional skills. The truth, of course, does not lie with the extreme of taking the opera to be a full-blown tragedy; nothing would be farther from the truth. But the other extreme of comprehending *Don Giovanni* as a pure *opera buffa* is equally perverted, and such an opinion cannot but be culled from the libretto alone, which, indeed, never transgresses the trifling language of a frivolous comedy. But Mozart lifted the characters of the play from the insignificant, yet typical, context. His demonic Don Giovanni, predestined by his nature to violence, sin, and final catastrophe, encounters a force which proves in the end to be the stronger: Donna Anna, who counteracts Don Giovanni to the ultimate destruction. And this is a demonic force, too, because of its perseverance in the pursuit of vengeance and just punishment. This contest of passion and virtue reverberates throughout the discords of human nature. It is a contest of demonic forces, as good and evil demons are given to man and no sharp boundary can tell where comedy ends and tragedy begins.

That our discussion has carried us but slightly beyond the margins of baroque opera will vex all those who cherish other idols, and put all expectation of a comprehensive summary to the foil. Are we then to omit the *Médée* of Cherubini; the rescue opera which the *Fidelio* made rightly and forever famous; Auber's *La Muette de Portici,* which not only culminated in a spectacular eruption of the volcanic Vesuvius, but when performed caused a political revolution to explode; Bellini's *Norma,* although Schopenhauer regarded the poignant "Qual cor tradisti" as the most tragic expression in music; *Les Troyennes* of Berlioz, the splendid display of tragedy inspired by the lofty mind of Virgil? Are we to omit the roll call of "tragic" operas which can be drawn out almost at random?

We are, indeed, and for good reasons. The baroque opera had laid so firm a foundation to operatic composition that, rooted in unalterable grounds, the changes of style affected the complexion, the conduct of operatic figures, but not the basic potential of dramatic expression in music. If Claudio Monteverdi and Alessandro Scarlatti set the two poles between which dramatic music wheeled, as I believe they did, Gluck's *Alceste* is an unconscious return to Monteverdi and Verdi's *Forza del Destino* an expansion of Scarlatti, with the two dramatic forces of Monteverdi and Scarlatti at last reconciled in *Otello,* Verdi's masterly and most stirring tragedy.

Yet we cannot omit the musical genius of the nineteenth century who, unlike Gluck, really set off an artistic revolution: Richard Wagner. Wagner was right in condemning the fallacies of operatic music as it had been composed by Spontini, Meyerbeer, or anyone else whom he attacked, and we would be even in agreement had the violent condemnation not come from the composer of *Rienzi,* the *Flying Dutchman,* or of *Tannhäuser,* which are of the same grain as the works at which he had a fling. Exactly there, on all the contradictions and inconsistencies, sit the difficulties which beset the freedom of our judgment.

The nature of our theme engages us to attend to the sole matter at hand: to the new concept of musical tragedy we are wont to impute to Wagner. The first thing that strikes our eyes on the path of this search is the fact that Wagner laid the theoretical groundwork for his new tragedy prior to any artistic accomplishment. This course of action though befitting a reformer is always startling when taken by an artist, and all the more so when we see that the art work to come obeyed the theory in all respects.

But this art work of the future, complete in design of substance and detail, solicited its vindication in the name of history. Possessed by the idea of necessity, Wagner set out to prove that the very shape of his music drama resulted from the compelling forces of historical evolution. Such proof, however, was not to be had just for the asking. There was but one way of coming into line with history: by distorting the facts whenever they disturbed the scheme. Any hurdle placed by a nasty composer on the course of history could always be leaped over or simply knocked down by the bold runner. But when it came to explain his own operas prior to the art work of the future, he had to double his acrobatic skills. At all events Wagner arrived at the coveted goal: the whole art of music, whether in the form of grand opera or of the symphony, had reached a dead end; hence the necessity of his music drama determining the future of art, as well as the necessity of forsaking all that music as an art had ever been.

He most emphatically asserted over and over again that his music drama had a meaning far beyond that of music alone. Not only would all the arts be merged in one greater total work of art, but the music drama was appointed to become Greek tragedy in a measure still vaster and more complete than the ancient model. Sensitive to the artistic virtues of Greek tragedy, he saw that among all the vital sources which richly sustained it, myth was the most powerful. The Nordic myth was to cloak the tragedy of Wagner.

However impetuously we might recoil from the fogginess of Teutonic myth, if tragedy and myth are as closely coupled as they are said to be, Wagner gave evidence of his keen insight when he linked his tragedy to myth—whatever its origin or nature. But in creating tragedy, he even presumed the role of the maker of myth. Just as he bent history to his purpose, he corrected the myth to suit his design. In the very midst of writing the libretti of his *Ring*, he drifted away from the true course of the saga for the sake of making his adjustments. We can understand why Nietzsche, with all justified amazement, marveled that Parsifal turned out to be the father of Lohengrin; he had every reason to exclaim: "How ever did he do it?" With myth distorted, the unending melody, which was the narrator of the story, and the leitmotiv, the perpetual label of all the mythical symbolisms that render music to mean more than music, forever divorced the Wagnerian drama from Greek tragedy—to say nothing of the Bayreuth Festspiele which, though intended to be the image of the Greek religious cult, became a monstrous farce of the Dionysian festival.

The expression of unbridled passion still remains the substance of the Wagnerian drama. *Tristan and Isolde* will continue to lay claim to the admiration of what its music means as music, and *Parsifal* may speak a language admired by some and rejected by others.

That musical tragedy had but one way of artistic expression, that of Wagner, was refuted in his own day. The proclamation that tragedy had been revised and revived did not affect the *Otello* of Verdi; nor did it silence Debussy.

But the aspect of Wagner's genius that held the most powerful grip over his time, that, though inspiring a host of composers, sapped artistic energies of many a musician— thus being the cause of tragic situations—will be among the themes of our final discourse.

V

The Tragic Pathos
in Music

What do we propose "tragic pathos" to purport? This is
no idle question if we allow ourselves at least for an instant
to reflect on the difference between the English and Greek
connotations of the word "pathos." In English, pathos is
said to denote an element or a quality in experience or
artistic expression, such as speech or writing, which evokes
or excites pity or compassion, or sadness; it is regarded as
an emotion of sympathetic pity. This meaning cannot but
take us by surprise, and we must marvel how the word
acquired the quality evocative of pity. For the Greek pathos
pertains to anything that befalls us, that has been inflicted
upon us from without, that we have suffered—hence the
significance of suffering, calamity, misfortune. It connotes
a passive condition of soul or of mind, emotions, passions,
and *pathemata* are such passive conditions brought into
being by the thrust of an outside force; the verb *paschein,*
pathein, also holds the passive element of being affected
from without. But while the noun "pathos" retains the
Greek word unchanged, the verb "to suffer" does not spring
from *pathein;* it derives from the Latin *sufferre,* to bear.

Now, I have no intention of making you suffer from the
pathos of semantics. I nevertheless should not fail to ask

why it is that in English pathos signifies an element that excites pity. And I venture, perhaps too boldly, to suggest that the connotation, estranged from the original, did not protrude from the Greek word pathos, but from the Greek tragedy, or rather from the Aristotelian definition that the tragedy must, in effect, cause or excite the two *pathemata* terror—and pity.

When I speak here of pathos, I shall not refer to the element which excites pity; rather I shall cling throughout to the Greek meaning of the word. It is true that the Greek verb *pathein* does not shut out the sense of being affected also by something good or positive, but such a sense must needs be specified by an additional indication. Without this, tacit inference of pathos will always infold the evil or the negative, consequently betoken suffering, sorrow, pain, sadness, melancholy, distress, agony. The impassioned as much as the pathetic appears to be marked by strong emotion. Hence, we shall search pith and marrow of these conditions wherever they bear upon musical expression outside the tragedy as a music drama or opera.

Now, do we not perpetrate the annoying blunder of redundancy if we attach the epithet of the "tragic" to the conditions of pathos? Is it not that outside the tragedy as a drama we always understand the tragic to mean sad, calamitous, distressing? If pathos speaks of suffering, does the tragic limit its scope or sharpen its meaning? If such were not the case, redundancy indeed should be frowned upon with patent disapproval.

But there are artistic forms expressive of a pathetic grain which came to life in response to an event or circumstance of the tragic hue, and there are others which have the cutting edge of tragic pathos without revealing its cause. On the one side, then, we light upon special compositions such as the plaintive song, dirge, complaint, *planctus*, which reflect a tragic incident, experience, or passion, and compositions which the tragic tenor of an age penetrated with the ring of melancholy tones. On the other side, we come face to face with compositions where for the discovery of the tragic pathos we must pry into their fabric. Let this distinction guide our further pursuits.

We are, indeed, in pursuit of *topoi*, of topics which summoned both poet and musician to voice the tragic pathos, and among these none other seems to be more closely allied to the scope of our case than the topic of the lament, the *planctus*, the mournful song bewailing the death of a person of eminence. Although descending by inheritance from ancient poetry, the medieval *planctus*, the lament par excellence, is not unlikely to have partaken in religious practices; originally, it even might have been part of the Office of the Dead, or included in the ceremonies at the burial.

The death of emperors and kings, men of high station, princes of the world and of the Church, the noblest minds of the time, kindled the creative imagination of the singer. Through the message of immortal art the awesome event would be known to the entire world; all mankind would mourn and join in singing the lament over the deplorable loss of a model of man, and his glory might outlive life itself. For the praiseworthy virtues of the dead bygone, the world appeared all the poorer. As grievous an affliction as the death of the great cloaked man and nature with the garb of mourning; it wakened the myriad voices of the universe to swell the wailing choir. Thus, sings the mourner his lament, the *planctus*—of Charlemagne, of William the

Conqueror, of Conrad II, the Emperor, of Philip Augustus, King of France, of Henry II, King of England. And the song was all the more woeful the more vividly the departed had invoked people's fancy, like the hero of a saga.

But the voice of the singer sounded sharpest when indignation spurred the lamenting to intensify his pathos, that is, when death occurred not as the natural end of man's journey, but by atrocious murder. Perhaps no other crime resounded in the medieval world of music as vehemently as the murder of Thomas à Becket, Archbishop of Canterbury, a crime the artistic echoes of which we still perceive in poetry and music of today. At the time when the gross offense was committed, the musician responded with the indignant accent of the whole western world in anger, and his lament over the dead trespassed the nature of the *planctus* because the violent tones of irate accusation hurled at those who instigated the murder drowned the plaintive modulation, though not the tragic pathos.

It would be erroneous were we to assume that the poet alone rendered the song with the force of a poignant utterance. The medieval singer often possessed both the rhythm of a poet and the melody of a musician, and only by the united powers of poetry and music did the work of art come to its completion. And that the medieval musician, even if now unknown by name, was capable of the stern, vindictive, emphatic diction which the expression of pathos demands can still be heard in the austerity of melodies renowned for their relentless grip.

The *planctus* was at times chosen to give vent to sorrow for a predicament other than the death of an eminent person. In "Ego flens ecclesia" the Church personified shed her tears in anguish over the schism and heretic aberrations. In the "Planctus Christi de malis praesulibus" Christ himself bewailed the woes which the corruptness of his vicars had brought upon all Christendom. In "Rahel plorat" Rachel wept in deep despair when she turned her thoughts to the Knights Templars, the fallen sons of the Church, accused of monstrous crimes and blasphemy. Her tears should rather have flown abundantly in sympathy with the poor wretches broken by cruel tortures and fatal punishment which Church and state conspired to wipe out the order in its entirety, an event of extreme tragedy which resounded throughout the world. Other musicians dedicated their motets to the defense of the Templars.

But lamenting the dead remained the principal function of the *planctus,* and so it continued through the ages. Sung with tragic pathos in awe of unsparing death it lived to sustain numberless changes, though never the loss of its solemn purpose. Man, predestined to death, thus had been ordained not to die in human memory. Over and again did the death of the great incite the artist to make his melancholy epitaph the equal of the tragic shock. The pathetic "Plourants" at the sarcophagus by the Burgundian sculptor Claus Sluter, mourners so powerfully real that even sculpture seemed capable of articulating an audible lament, appear like precursors, carved in stone, of "Cueurs desolez par toutes nations," rendered in sound, probably by Pierre de la Rue. Disconsolate hearts mourning all the world over compose, indeed, a choir of "Plourants" whose somber voices weave the grievous song around the austere *Dies illa, dies irae,* most fittingly chosen from *Libera me* of the Office of the Dead to be the nerve of the musical structure. And just as the sculptured weepers captured the lament at the crest of the emotional surge, so did the music ring with the quintessence of the melancholy *planctus*. Another lament of striking resemblance in structure and mood, based on the same text "Cueurs desolez par toutes nations" but joined to the chant "Plorans ploravit in nocte," might well be the contribution of Josquin des Prés to the same unknown event. Yet we know the event which invited the lamenting voice of Heinrich Isaac in two motets of equal grandeur: the death of Lorenzo il Magnifico de' Medici.

It was not always and only the death of men eminent by their station which moved the composer to fancy tones for expressing anguish and pathos. Many a *planctus* had been dedicated to musicians upon their death by fellow composers, and the *Déploration* which Josquin wrote in memory of Okeghem is for its artistic perfection and intensity among the worthiest.

The poem of Monteverdi's famous cycle "Lagrime d'Amante al Sepolcro dell' Amata," Tears of the Lover at the Tomb of the Beloved, is nothing more than the stylish tale of the shepherd in grief over the loss of his nymph. Yet his work was, in fact, a *planctus* for the celebrated singer Caterina Martinelli who, chosen to sing the part of Ariadne, had died at the age of eighteen shortly before the first performance of the music drama. Monteverdi sang his poignant lament in her honor in the guise of a pastoral story. Teeming with new structural conceits and driven by his passion of having artistic forms disengage emotions from their natural lack of precision, he invested the *planctus* with the fullness of his new efforts. And here again, he tested the depth of his subject not for the obvious meaning of words, but for their human implications, the drift of which he measured with the prodigious gauge of his vision.

Just as the medieval *planctus* might have risen from the

pristine source of the liturgical services for the dead, so at one time of its history it returned to the fold of liturgy, and in a manner both strange and noteworthy. I have in mind the *Musical Exequies* of Heinrich Schütz and their unusual origin. The story is known. A patron of the musician, Heinrich Posthumus, sovereign of Reuss, while still alive ordered his coffin made, with biblical passages of his own choice inscribed. Chosen with a view to his own funeral service, the texts of hope of ultimate salvation formed an organic unity, reflecting a consistent liturgy and inspiring artistic entirety. He then charged the composer to set his music to the biblical passages. Thus, an epitaph engraved changed its substance into sound. And rendered in the shape of liturgy, the lament of the dead became a requiem, but one of personal invention. When Schütz recommended that the work, once it had served its purpose at the funeral, be also sung as the Mass at the feast of purification of Mary the Virgin and on the Sixteenth Sunday after Trinity, he markedly strengthened the liturgical aspect. But precisely this conversion of the *planctus* into liturgical music divested the artistic pathos of the tragic shroud as death had lost its painful sting.

A striking likeness pertains to Bach's cantata "Gottes Zeit ist die allerbeste Zeit" (106) which, too, was suggested as liturgical music for the sixteenth Sunday after Trinity. But the cantata had to be detached from its origin if it were to find a new place in liturgy. For Bach composed it for the funeral of a distinguished, though unknown, person in Weimar. And he even called his work an *Actus tragicus*, no doubt on the grounds that the lament of the dead must needs be an act of tragic pathos. But where does the tragic element remain if the composition is lifted into a sphere of serenity which is not the sphere of death, the merciless reaper, unless his dreadful harvest is thought to bring about the mercy of redemption? Bach's cantata might be an *Actus tragicus* as long as it is understood to be a *planctus*, a lament of the dead; it loses its claim to the title if it becomes music of religious edification within the frame of liturgy, for religion with its beacon of hope assuaged the sharpness of the tragic.

The shift, however remarkable, of the *planctus*—and let the lament of the dead still thus be called to signify the *topos*—from the sorrowful event which determined its origin to a completely new liturgical function was never more than the exception. Even contact with religious thoughts came to be relaxed and cast aside at last in modern times. Not that thereby the *planctus* vanished altogether from the set of topics of the tragic pathos in music; it still reverberates today. Hindemith designed his *Trauermusik* to mourn over the death of King George V of England; Stravinsky wrote his dirge in memory of the poet Dylan Thomas; and when Prince Fürstenberg died, Pierre Boulez composed his gripping *planctus* named "Tombeau," with the verse of Mallarmé "Un peu profond ruisseau calomnié la mort" being the inscription of the sounding tomb, the final part of *Pli selon pli*.

Now, is it not that the requiem, the official liturgy of the dead, would appear to constitute a culmination of the *planctus*, and all the more as many a time, if not always, it came to be composed in sympathetic response to the death of prominent men? Being first and foremost a prayer service for the deceased to the Redeemer, it hardly could become the highest fulfillment of the lament. And yet, despite every reverence to the liturgical nature of prayer for final salva-

tion, the appalling text of *Dies irae* with its direful stanzas
"Tuba mirum," "Rex tremendae majestatis," "Lacrymosa
dies illa," as well as the anxieties of the last *Libera me*,
"seized with fear and trembling," stirred all deep-seated
powers of the musician to keep artistic expression of the
tragic pathos abreast with the terrible cries of man on the
day of the Last Judgment. It is true that older compositions
of the requiem shunned the realistic outburst of subjective
emotions and that the mass of the dead incorporated the
Dies irae relatively late; nevertheless they adapted the elements of structure, harmony, and color to the pathos of the
text on their own aesthetic grounds; and the choral requiem
of Pierre de la Rue, to name but one, with its dark voices,
the deepest ever written for a chorus, captured the tenebrous
pathos by the gloom of tonal color and uncommon harmonies.

But the subjective expression of tragic pathos did, indeed, emerge from the vastly deep of the individual's feeling, though only in the requiem of modern times. The
composition might still be a commissioned work, like that
of Mozart. Yet personal circumstances began decisively to
play upon its origin, circumstances which at times were
forceful enough to bear upon the subjective shape so heavily
that the work disengaged itself from the embrace of the
liturgy. The melancholy remnant of Mozart's Requiem,
sublime, but for the added touches by unskilled hands and
simple minds imperfect, had its tones of tragic pathos
sharpened by the composer's own nearness to death and by
the sorrows of his last troubled years.

The liturgical frame, however, was completely broken
by the stupendous requiem which Berlioz composed upon
request and conducted in the Dôme des Invalides at the

memorial service for the soldiers killed in action while taking possession of Constantine. With one large and four small orchestras and a chorus of 400 which, space permitting, might be doubled, Berlioz depicted the Last Judgment as a musical fresco of gigantic dimensions as though his strained concept of terror and pathos, of grief felt in the veins of his own self, could only be equalled by the immensity of means. The overwhelming profusion of sound effects, the grandiose and the pathetic, the sweeping strokes of the boldest realism enthralled an Alfred de Vigny, the profoundly musical poet and friend of Berlioz; together with a host of romantics he was smitten by a music savage, convulsive, yet grievous, and not at all the less beautiful. But the utterance of the composer's inner self, disclosing his pathetic feeling and experience, the personal confession, sounds still above the monumental size.

Indeed, the romantic conceit of molding the work of art in response to the urge of subjective expression marked all the modern compositions of the requiem with the personal seal of individualism; and none other attested to its drift more candidly than the German Requiem of Brahms. It may well be that Brahms's work had been inspired by the death of Schumann or even Schumann's own intention to compose a German Requiem which never came to pass. At all events, it was many years after Schumann's death that Brahms completed his work. And it was decidedly a requiem of his own making, first of all because of the compound of texts which though chosen from the Bible mirrored an extraordinarily personal view. And precisely this personal interpretation, bent on hope, consolation, and promise rather than on unabated despair, relentless nemesis, or the inexorable last reckoning, deprived Brahms's Requiem not of the pitiful tones of lament and misery, but of the austere mode of the tragic pathos, regardless of its complete removal from the realm of liturgy. It is an art work, profoundly sad, a personal expression, but never a contribution to a religious service of the dead, nor anything else but a work of art with tones of compassion, yet not of tragic terror.

The greatest requiem of the nineteenth century, the *Messa da Requiem* of Verdi, affirmed soaring individualism not in the least restricted, although the work was based on the official text of the liturgy. Known for his distant attitude toward the Church, Verdi had never been drawn in earnest to religious music except for a short phase of his youth. When he learned that Alessandro Manzoni, Italy's noblest poet of the time and his admired friend, had been stricken by adversity and grief, he thought that Divine Providence should it really exist would never have inflicted such a tribulation on such a saintly man. Verdi had once suggested that the most renowned Italian musicians should muster up their artistic energies for a requiem to be composed jointly in honor of Rossini, and he, in fact, completed the final part of *Libera me*. But Verdi's proposal, which came to nought, was stimulated by a patriotic, not religious, intent. And there the matter rested unfinished. In 1871 Verdi declared that in view of numberless masses of the dead it would be senseless to add one more to the supply already plentiful.

Two years later Alessandro Manzoni died. Deeply hurt by the death of his great friend, Verdi at once resolved to compose a requiem in reverence to the poet. Thus, stabbed by the pangs of his own suffering, he built the monumental tomb lamenting over sorrow that was loud and long. When first performed in the San Marco at Milan, the requiem accorded with the character of a memorial service as an appropriate tribute to the poet. But Verdi cast for his personal confession of the tragic pathos, this masterwork of a subjective explication of the text, the frame of the public concert, and within this frame it continued to keep its rightful place.

Among the laments in use during the twelfth and earlier part of the thirteenth centuries we meet with a group of songs entitled *Planctus Christi morientis,* the lament which pouring from the lips of the dying Christ appeals to all mankind. Christ nailed to the cross, himself the singer wailing in pain, sings his admonition: "Homo, vide, quae pro te patior," Man, behold what I suffer for thee. This mournful song, no doubt, had been inspired by a great model, the Improperia, the Reproaches which Christ uttered from the cross: "My people, what have I done to thee? Answer me," and they belong to the liturgy of Good Friday.

Searching the vast province of *topoi,* of topics which roused the musician's fancy to mold the tragic pathos in artistic shapes, we shall hardly invade a climate more charged with the potential of the tragic than when we come upon the liturgies of Holy Week and Lent. The penitential psalms, the Improperia, the Lamentations of Jeremiah, and above all the Passion of Christ, all had their theme of tragedy, of sadness and suffering, pronounced with the sting that provokes the artist. We shall not weigh, as we have said before, the religious gravity of the themes since the idea of redemption, inherent in all of them, deflects the tragic from its true course. For the tragic when taking its run does not promise either mercy or hope.

Although wrapped alike in the same liturgy and to the same degree imprinted deeply by the grievous story of

Christ's suffering, the themes invited the imagination of the artist with divergent force, and the response of the musician had been accordingly diversified. Is it not strange that such poignant exclamations as "behold and see if there be any sorrow like unto my sorrow," or "all kindreds of the earth shall wail because of him," did not at once call forth an echo as piercing as the original voice? In fact, the echo was late in forthcoming, whether it issued from the Improperia, the Lamentations, or the Passion; and well it may be that the liturgical restrictions imposed by the mournful season prevented the musician from matching his force of expression with the force of the theme. At all events, it is noteworthy that musicians of the Renaissance, and even the greatest among them, seem to have stood aloof from the theme, and when they committed themselves to the task, they abode by a simplicity of structure and a primitivity of style which they did not allow to be set forth in any of their other compositions. True it is that Palestrina's Improperia still caught the awful emotion by simplicity and directness, but it is not the artistic effort strained to the extreme of its capacity which bears upon the musical form. Nor can the doleful calmness of the work be said to ring with the passionate vibrations of the tragic pathos which the dramatic text convokes. In compliance with the lugubrious service, somber hues portrayed the general mood rather than the particular characteristics of the text.

The Lamentations of Jeremiah, whose stirring outcries over the destruction of Jerusalem and the Temple as well as the calamities of the Jewish people should be expected most strongly to appeal to the creative mind of the musician, at first did not engage the abilities which the composer had shown elsewhere. Even renowned musicians held back their skills and often resorted to completely artless designs, if not obsolete techniques. It is as though when shaping the Lamentations the composer worked on a different plane, admitting of no complex devices which through their organizing power would beget a cast at once intricately wrought.

Yet surprise must needs ensue when we observe that only the music for the Hebrew letters was allowed to ascend to the height of greater refinement, though not to the summit of artistic resources, while the music to the poignant texts of the lamentations themselves stood by the frugal fare of psalmodic recitation. Thus, the musical shape runs counter, as it were, to all expectations: where the text, the Hebrew letters, showed indifference to the tragic theme, the music was elaborate, if not expressive, and where the text amassed the tragic pathos, the music recited the lamentation with tones, though somewhat emphatic, nonetheless restrained. The numerous Lamentations of Palestrina neither altered nor expanded the basic plan of composition; and his adherence to the prescript of tradition had certainly been watched by the ecclesiastic authorities in Rome. However compliant with the mandate of liturgy, Palestrina succeeded here and there in permeating the simple structure with tones germane to the mood of sorrow. But musicians far from the zealous guardians of the Vatican did not forsake the traditional simplicity even if they were unable to make simplicity synonymous with profundity. Only Orlando di Lasso, a deeply melancholy mind, seems to have inflected his voice of lamentation more sharply to the nature of the text.

Most surprising are the early compositions of the Passion. Whether they are *Motetti de passione* or complete in the presentation of Christ's passion, they all seem to be formed not by a composer incited to be the interpreter of tragic events as much as by a narrator called upon to recount a sad story with a subdued voice. Surely, there are differences of greatness, but the differences are the shades in the art of narration, not of interpretation. And when it comes to give an account of the climax of the story, the pitiful death of Christ, the voice of the narrator may tremble, but the account remains within the realm of recitation and its epic, not the realm of tragic rhetoric.

Cipriano de Rore, surely a composer who knew how to express human emotions, in his Passion is only the narrator of a pathetic story, not the interpreter of pathos; and if the compositions of Orlando di Lasso or Victoria are more moving, the deeper effect comes merely from raising the pitch of narration. Here again, the liturgical restrictions imposed upon the composer the need for artistic restraint which kept his will to strive after expressive eloquence within the narrowest bounds.

During the whole period of the Renaissance, then, the very theme which like none other was fraught with pathos failed to find commensurate expression for reasons other than artistic, yet not for want of masterly minds. Within the frame of the individual motet the composer set free all his powers of art even if he dealt with the subject of Christ's suffering. The pathos of Lassus' *Tristis est anima mea*, the words of Christ uttered when in the garden of Gethsemane, surpassed all that the music of the Passion proper was permitted to express. If we draw our conclusions only from the music of the Improperia, the Passion, or the Lamentations of Jeremiah, we will obtain a distorted picture suggestive even of the musician's complete incapacity to shape the tragic pathos.

There are, however, other topics which freely carried the musician of the Renaissance on the wings of fancy to the utterance of pathos: penitential psalms such as "Miserere mei, Deus, secundum misericordiam tuam," Have mercy on me, o God, according to thy mercy; "De profundis clamavi ad te Domine," Out of the depths I cry unto thee; the lament of David over Saul and Jonathan, "Planxit autem David"; or David's lament over the death of his son, "Absalom, fili mihi." In these musicians such as Josquin des Prés rose to the full height of their artistic capacities. New structures invented to match the pathetic nature of the theme as well as new modulations adapted to the meaning of the words were employed to voice tragic pathos. These themes, rather than the Passion, were sharply incentive and capable of pressing even minor artists forward beyond their ordinary faculty of speech. This Tomkins, a conservative musician, proved with his motet "When David heard that Absalom was slain."

Yet what the musician of the Renaissance gave as an expression of the tragic pathos had never been an outburst of emotion, much less a personal confession. A remarkable singularity of structure, an unexampled subtlety of tonal organization, a boldness in chromatic harmonies—this was about all he allowed to testify to the pathos of the theme. Josquin's fiftieth psalm *Miserere mei* or his laments of David made history not by their effusion of personal feelings, but by the eminence of their structure. Hence all the compositions of the Renaissance, even when unmistakably tuned to the expression of the tragic pathos, retain the aloofness of objectivity which separates the presentation of a theme from the utterance of the composer's emotion.

On these very grounds, however, modern times, which start with the baroque, and old music, which ends with Palestrina, part company forever. For it is there and then that the expressiveness of affection prevailed over the mere presentation of themes. And there and then it occurred that the poignancy of tragic pathos, inherent in the Passion, the Improperia, and the Lamentations of Jeremiah, came to be touched by new artistic aspirations.

"Movere gli affetti," to move human affections, now the ultimate purpose of music, the supreme among all ambitions of the artist, quickened the endeavors and led the composition on its course. The goal, however, cannot be reached unless musicians subject their work, each individual composition, to the task of presenting affections. It is to be noted that the baroque composer took an affection, an emotion, in the most literal, nearly physical, sense as something that is agitated, active, in motion; and such an understanding was bound to impart to music the element of the dramatic, as action predicates drama.

That the baroque had traveled on its new path fast and far away from the past might be inferred if we compare two motets based on the same pathetic text, the Lament of David over Absalom, both of grandeur and peerless excellence, but each in a world of its own. Josquin's *Absalom, fili mi* renders pathos as a frame of mind, as an intrinsic mood, which pervades the work as a whole with persevering intensity. In his *Fili mi, Absalom* Heinrich Schütz sets the affection of the tragic pathos in motion, as it were, to rise from the deep of human pain into the open. The surging melody of the solo voice, accompanied by four trombones symbolic of the lament, breaks into piercing outcries "per te moriar, moriar, moriar," repeated precipitately over and again.

This is no mood of melancholy, nor the state of suffering, but affection propelled with the forward thrust of action. If tragic pathos comes to be the theme of composition, it will be fomented from now on by this concept of affection and expressiveness. And since the style of baroque music shaped its vocabulary—idiomatic of the utterances of affections—together with the music drama or opera, religious music of the baroque fell completely under the sway of the secular idiom. But the stimulant of moving human affections lost nothing of its force on account of the religious purpose. On the contrary, it empowered the composer of vision to interpret human connotations of sacred texts and thereby to bring concealed truth closer to the human grasp.

Thus, trying themes chosen from the book of Job, or Psalms of anguish, attracted the musician with a new force to lift affections from the themes and cast them into the new language of musical pathos. Even the liturgies of Holy Week did not bend aside his natural proclivity to implant all the topics of the tragic in the elements of the new style. It must be said, however, that the ecclesiastic interdiction of using instruments during the services of Holy Week had not at once been disobeyed. To our knowledge the Capella Sistina never violated the rule, though elsewhere in Italy and in other countries, Protestant as well as Catholic, musicians did not waive the claim of instrumental music to its appurtenant share in modulating the affections to the full range of the style.

François Couperin drew instruments into his famous Leçons de Ténèbres for the matins of Maundy Thursday,

Good Friday, and Holy Saturday, and so did Francesco Durante. Alessandro Scarlatti employed an orchestra in his remarkable Passion, faithfully abiding by the Gospel of St. John, a work which has been oddly neglected, even mis-judged, yet was rightly admired by Claude Debussy. The last witness to the power of inspiration which flowed forth from the Lamentations of Jeremiah made its appearance with the Threni of Stravinsky, religious in character, but not liturgical, with his selection of the texts deviating from the official formulary. This work is a testimony to artistic greatness, not only because of its extraordinary structure, built upon a model of Webern, but also for its aesthetic complexity; in fact it is a testimonial to the tragic pathos the impact of which emerges mainly from his bold essay at refurbishing Hebrew cantillation.

The story of Christ's Passion now infused into the mind of the composer even the power of inventing new artistic forms. Heinrich Schütz combined the seven words Christ spoke on the cross to bring them into relief within one composition. Not that this was the first time the seven words were united by harmonizing the Gospels. But Schütz, animated by the spirit of the dramatic *stile concertante*, was first in bringing about a new musical category with which he approached the oratorio. A full oratorio, complete with solo arias, ensembles, and orchestral compositions, sprouted from the story of the passion with the new baroque *Sepolcro* which, in its early phase, was even presented with scenic display. And I believe that the curiously dramatic, if not theatrical, first performance of Haydn's *Seven Words of Christ at the Cross* in Cadiz in Spain, from where the com-mission to compose the work had come, was fashioned by previous customs of staging the *Sepolcro*.

The baroque oratorio wholly prevailed over the shape of the Passion, and as a consequence the Gospel was replaced by new poetic texts. But the three Passions of Schütz, composed toward the end of his life, stand entirely apart. Schütz still held fast to the Gospel; he conspicuously precluded elements of the oratorio and rejected instrumental accompaniment of any kind; he created a new chantlike recitation. Thus, he committed the pathos of his austere and sagacious disclosure of the tragic to the human voice alone. Surely, this grandiose austerity speaks of his insistence on the liturgical significance of the Passion, but his insistence came in a period when the perception of liturgical exigency was out of joint with the time. Yet the Passions of Schütz towered above the rest in complete isolation not only for their liturgical integrity, but for their artistic form as well. No echo came from these monumental works which, neither heard nor seen, remained in tragic solitude until, of late, their unique worthiness had been discovered. And strange it is, indeed, that a similar fate of tragic isolation also overtook the masterwork, the sum and substance of the opposite artistic form, the oratorio-passions of Bach which, no longer in harmony with their time, were denied even the scantiest effect and at once unjustly buried in oblivion. But there we touch upon our final theme: the tragic fate of the musician.

Is there, then, outside the realm of the music drama, and besides the various forms of the *planctus*, the lament, no other topic within the province of secular music which released the composer's intent to express the tragic pathos? In the vast region of secular expressions, predominant even in certain phases of the Middle Ages, to say nothing of more modern times, did no other theme lead to the artistic configuration of the tragic? Is it not that medieval lyrics, the madrigal of the Renaissance, never cease to reverberate the plaintive song over the tortures of love which, unrequited, makes death more desirable than life? Mysterious as it might be, love, at least in lyrics, seems rarely to have been rewarded with what the lover's efforts made bold to seek, and his song reiterated "the music, yearning like a God in pain" (Keats).

There is no end to the complaint over the tortures of love, no end to sighs and tears over love left without answer, no end to longing for death if the passionate voice of love should meet with no response. "Weepe, weepe, mine eyes," the aches of the "woeful heart," "Malheureux cueur," "Plaine de dueil," "Io piango," "O death rock me asleep," in short, torments, suffering, death, echo and re-echo in every line of amorous lyrics. Every singer believes himself justified to sing: "J'ai bien cause de lamenter," I have good reason to lament. Love and death speak with the voices of a strange companionship, and the more deeply we become immersed in the lyrics of the declining Middle Ages, the more monotonously sound the strains of melancholy. "Je ris en pleurs," Weeping I laugh—the line of irony, of conflicting emotions, of melancholy as an ever present mood, is not the verse of François Villon alone; it is the language of amorous poetry of a whole age.

Now does the image which mingles death and love really mirror death with the sharpness of its final sting? What is the meaning of the strange line: Let me die while I am living, until death comes? The French are wont to name the ecstatic consummation of amorous embrace "la petite mort"; and it is this "little" death, rather than the great and last, that appears as the companion of love.

But if we attempt to penetrate to the genuine core of all these laments, to the sincerity of torment and suffering, the sincerity of the tragic pathos, we will find it is easier to grasp the wonders of intuitive poetry than to pierce the heavy shield of conventions, style, and the rigid code of manners and morals which covered all directness of expression. It is true that musicians brought the lament over the tortures of love to the height of tragic pathos. They made tears audible where they were not even visible. But the musician's voice was no less servant to a stern code than the voice of the poet. And only in modern times initiated by the baroque composer did it come to pass that the musician lamented his own sorrows and distress, that the tragic pathos of the *Winterreise* emanated from the "Malheureux cueur" of Schubert.

So far, all artistic expressions of the tragic pathos seem to have been inevitably intertwined with an incident or an occasion, either real or poetically feigned, which conveyed the theme of grief and affliction to the artist. Thus, the initial motive which, with varying force, induced the musician to image the pathetic themes did not lie within himself. He, nevertheless, might have followed a natural bent when he chose the themes from poetry, with this bias being contingent either upon the temper of his time or upon his own innate disposition.

And all the sounds of the tragic pathos that were neither suggested nor stimulated by an outside motive emerged from the deep well of the artist's nature. Mozart's profoundly tragic Kyrie of the C-minor Mass is not merely a transfiguration of the text; rather it is the disconsolate utterance of his own self, of his own tragic being, and to no lesser degree personal than his D-minor Quartet, seizing with its terror and despair. And Schubert's *Wegweiser*, no less than the Adagio of his string Quintet is a revelation of his own despondency and melancholy immeasurable for its complete hopelessness.

And this anticipates our last theme: Tragic Figures in Music.

VI

Tragic Figures in Music

Marcel Proust once said: "As for happiness, it has nearly one advantage only, that of making unhappiness possible. When in happiness, we must establish bonds, very sweet and very strong in confidence and attachments in order that their rupture causes us that tribulation, so precious, which is called unhappiness." Why does unhappiness with all the painful sorrows of the heart deserve so high a praise as to be precious? Is grief, despite its dreadful aches, a blessing, divine, and to be welcomed? It is, indeed; for, to continue with Proust, "happiness is wholesome only for the body, but it is heartache that develops the forces of the mind."

Sorrow, the maker of man, of the great, of the artist, must be accepted as the most potent leaven of creative work. It opens the eye of the mind, with the vision suddenly sharpened and casting about its rays, as it were, in the infinite realm of the dark and the deep where images take shape, the fruits of suffering reaped by the "woe-illumed mind" (Shelley).

But these images, molded in the "delirium of lucidity" (Paul Valéry), are not ephemeral emotions, however thoroughly they have been tinged by human values; rather they are, in their finite clarity, visionary configurations of the artistic work itself: patterns, symbols, forms, and motives which effect artistic structures. These "öbere Eingiessungen," as Dürer called them, influences from above, influxes divine, beget the concrete shapes, geometrical for Dürer as he assumed true painters to abound with figures within themselves. If critics of today reproach modern musicians for calculating mathematical formulas, they forget or do not know that precisely these forms determining musical composition—as they do as much in the present as they did in the past—are divine influences like the geometrical configurations of Dürer.

"Why is it," Aristotle asked in his *Problemata*, "that all those who have become eminent in philosophy, or politics, or poetry, or the arts are apparently melancholics, of an atrabilious temperament, and some of them to such an extent as to be affected by diseases caused by black bile, as is said to have happened to Heracles among the heroes? For he appears to have been of this nature wherefore epileptic afflictions were called by the ancients 'the sacred disease' after him." "And many others of the heroes seem to have been similarly afflicted, and among men of recent times Empedocles, Plato, and Socrates, and numerous other well-known men, and also most of the poets." "All melancholics have remarkable gifts, not owing to disease but from natural causes." Thus, Aristotle defined atrabilious physiology to be the temperament of all "inspired persons," as he said, who accomplish the extraordinary. And do we not take the atrabilious still to be synonymous with the melancholy, the hypochondriac?

Melancholy, then, appears to be the preordained temper of genius, innate like a womb from which creative work ascends, the permanent companion of all creative vision. And if the melancholy frame of mind, the matrix of creation, can never be without torment and sorrow, we understand why men of genius have hailed "melancholia generosa," why artists down to T. S. Eliot and Schönberg blessed unhappiness and, in the end, embraced their torturers. "La mia allegrezz' è la malinconia," My gladness is melancholy: this utterance of Michelangelo betrays bliss flowing, as it does, from suffering.

But then, by the law of reason, all artists seem destined to be tragic figures; and, essentially, this must be true, even if we are unable to furnish biographical proof for each and every individual. Yet our quest for tragic figures in music cannot be satisfied with a universal assumption of tragedy. Hence let us consider historic constellations which forced a tragic complexion upon musicians, and let us reflect on the demonic, the Promethean, the romantic, the modern tragic figure.

Whatever view we take of the tragic, it seems that the Middle Ages never allowed the tragic musician to manifest himself. If this is so, we still wonder whether he did not exist. Is it that convention, style, and a rigid code of life put upon the face of all composers, of all artists, the mask which safely hid their human selves? And was the mask an instrument of coercion for the artist to endure, or a welcome shield which permitted appearance without commitment? Were we able to pierce the mask without harm to the substance behind it, we could not be certain that we should find the real face to be wholly different from the mask. For the mask and all that it covers may well be one and the same. Such are the powers of style, a safeguard of man and his life, that substance and appearance merge forever in a solid compact.

Nevertheless, an age that teemed with the strongest individualities, powerful in mind and in action, towering high above all common measures, bound to have their aspirations run against adversaries; an age that has been tried perpetually by the austere tensions between the *vita activa* and *vita contemplativa*, with the active life swiftly moving into entanglements, corruption, baseness, imperfections, and defilement, in short, into violation of all the spiritual commands of Providence, and with the contemplative life, the only one that could be said to answer man's appointed purpose, calling for retreat from the world into the solitude of readiness for the final retribution—such an age, I say, cannot but infold the propensity to the tragic conditions of human existence. The tragic conditions of the mind incited those sharp conflicts which have been recorded in the glorious documents of human achievement; but rarely are we allowed to perceive the document's author—such as Abelard for instance—as a tragic figure.

Though among the literati the tragedy of mind suggests at least from time to time a human tragedy, artists, above all musicians, never rise to bring the shape of the tragic individual into sight. This is a result, in part, of the loss of records. What manner of man was a Léonin, a Pérotin, a Pierre de la Croix? These are surely all men of extraordinary genius, powerful minds, inventive vision, and individuality. And what of Petrarch's intimate friend, Philippe de Vitry, poet and musician, statesman, philosopher, man of the Church, who sharply voiced in his musical work his fierce reactions to events of the time or to his adversaries? Of profound thought and violent passion, so deeply involved in the tragic conditions of the *vita activa*, he must have been among the tragic figures of a tumultuous era, for us only to be divined with all the uncertainty of a conjecture.

But next to him we descry an older musician, Jacques de

Liège, the most comprehensive of universal minds in all matters musical, whom a historical situation rendered a tragic figure. It is by the conflict between old and new, between an *ars antiqua* and an *ars nova*, between the two generations of fathers and sons, that the man was painfully troubled. Because of his *amor musicae*, he loved the younger musicians even though intellectually he opposed their doctrine; because of his old age, he knew that he would be the loser, for right stands at the side of youth outliving the old. Swayed from approval of feeling to disapproval of mind he saw himself forced into the tragic situation of conflict, into a crisis which accrues whenever a younger generation injects a new style in the order of old.

We are wont to expect autobiography to be the golden bridge which leads us promptly into the heart of the artist, thus unraveling the mystery at last. The first autobiography a musician ever wrote dates from the fourteenth century, and it is of Guillaume de Machaut. But expectations will be frustrate. For Guillaume de Machaut records events of his life in the light of courtly glamour and adventure like an impartial chronicler, and though the record is not devoid of a personal ring, he still draws an impenetrable veil of style and of convention over the artist's personality. Good reasons lead us to surmise that in his age of frightful stresses he must have been first in being exposed to tragic situations. It is not, however, from his autobiography, not from his *Livre du Voir Dit*, his "Dichtung und Wahrheit," Fiction and Truth, but from his music and poetry that we rake the evidence of his tragic being. Yet is it his own or that of his time? For the tone of melancholy pervades all that he composed, and it sounds as though it echoed the cultural climate of the declining Middle Ages, rather than the singular grief of a personal tragedy.

In fact, mental and emotional disturbances sapped more and more the foundations of the age. Harsh clashes between reality of life and a pronounced ideal, between extreme depravity and excessive piety; the constant fear of the final holocaust, the Last Judgment; the contrast of vice and virtue, of the sublime and the vile, of splendor and misery—all this engendered a climate of pessimism the like of which is heard but at the end of time. And the further we advance into the fifteenth century, the darker all colors become. An age of pain, of tears, of horrors, of falsehood and condemnation, an age of sadness and of gloom: thus poets voiced their weariness of life, and all had learned to fear the frowns of fortune.

"Tous cueurs ont prins par assaut / Tristesse et merencolie"; All hearts are assailed by the blows of sadness and melancholy. And so it seems that melancholy under the fits of which man smarted without release, permeated all minds and grew to be the "maladie du siècle," the disease of the time. "La fin s'approche, en vérité," In truth, the end is near (Deschamps). Of causes there were many substantiated enough to justify the pessimistic frame of mind. But despite the authenticity of gloom in this "age of darkness," we still perceive the accents of a vogue which sound in unison with the tale of pessimism. And precisely because of the conventions of a style in vogue do we fail safely to assess the effect of melancholy on shaping the tragic element in the individual. Musicians such as Dufay and Binchois, no doubt, reverberated the melancholy strains of the age, but without exposing the artist fully as a tragic figure. Never are we so certain about the tragic texture of historical conditions, and never are we so uncertain in trying to grasp the tragic nature of the artist.

Composers burdened with the tragic fate of being born under unfavorable conditions are not so rare as we might be ready to assume. It often occurred that a tragic discord issued from a situation where an artist, cast by his lot into peripheral remoteness far distant from the center of art, from the core of things, would find himself in the great deep of uncertainty about the drift of style, about the decisive idiom of the time; and no greatness, if born under such conditions, seems to have been great enough to upset the historical order in its own favor.

The baroque would appear to abound with tragedies which, though "impersonal," that is, effected by the conditions of the time, were no less deeply felt by the individual. As the constellation of the baroque style was fixed by Italian composers and by the secular spirit of the music drama, musicians of countries other than Italy, unable to probe the pulse of the time, came to work under the cloud of tragic insecurity. And no other country inflicted musicians with harsher tragedies than Germany where, prior to the rise of the baroque, religious music, Netherlandish in provenance and in the shape of choral polyphony, was held supreme. But when the new European style of music came to be formed by Italians and fashioned by a secular spirit, religious music submerged or yielded to the sweep of the profane. Wherever, as in Germany, all musical forces at first held fast to tradition, but also were attracted to the novelties of Italy, a situation, confusing and conflicting, arose which had all shapes of tragedy in store. How is the tradition of religious music to be reconciled to the secular tenor of Italian baroque? And how is the soloistic art of the new Italian opera to be harmonized with musical organizations which were tuned to the choral medium of sacred polyphony? These questions reflect the incongruities of German music in the age of the baroque; and the incongruities were responsible for the tragedy of the individual.

None recognized the complete transformation of European music, of its purpose as well as its style, with a keener eye than Heinrich Schütz, and none penetrated more deeply the meaning of the momentous change and the nature of the new music. Although he drew his knowledge of the new trend from the very source in Italy, upon return to Germany he attuned the new designs of composition to religious rather than secular music. Despite the shift from the profane to the sacred, Schütz did not alter the composer's function of revealing human affections, the human substance of religious texts; in this, he and his Italian model were in harmony.

But the shift speaks also of the mission of his work. Bent on sustaining religious tradition, he clearly foresaw that German music would be doomed to the backwardness of provincialism unless the whole organic structure of musical life could be renewed by an agreement with Italian art. There he conceived his mission to lie. Yet in the end his mission came to nought. The greater the height he reached with his work by his efforts, the greater the distance, the sharper the tensions, between genius and environment; and the more perfect the accomplishment, the more painful its isolation. For the first time, at least in German music, the historical situation showed genius and surroundings to have become disjoined, with no communication, no interchange on common grounds. In the tragic seclusion of his last years,

Schütz completed his work, only to see it promptly buried and forgotten. In the end he cursed the day when he turned to the profession of music instead of following his bent for the study of humanities. Thus, Schütz conceded with the bitterness of a tragic artist the fruitlessness of a sublime effort.

Fate gathering its force from historical conditions repeated the tragedy of Schütz with the appearance of J. S. Bach, for similar reasons and with the same result. While the kinship of middling musicians and their contemporaries continued to flourish without disturbance, the discord between the great artist, the genius, and his environment had grown to be sharper and more poignant at the time of Bach. To ascertain what isolation, futility, forgottenness of an artistic work, meant in the age of German baroque, we need but broach the question what Bach knew of Schütz. No more, it seems, than the psalter of Becker, works, then, which were not even designed by artistic aspiration. Oblivion succeeded in performing its deadening effect, and even Bach, though raised under the most favorable conditions of musical craft, got no inkling of his great predecessor.

And he, too, would be stricken by the fate of being forgotten before death. For a while it looked as though he would free himself from the fetters of provincialism. But when he accepted the position of cantor at Leipzig, he saw his work increasingly hemmed in within the narrowest of local confines, and shortsightedness, want of comprehension, blindness to artistic values, began to blight his aspiration and his music. All he set forth deliberately to improve the state of music met with indifference or outright rejection. No wonder that from time to time he burst out into utterances of wrath and indignation, yet without avail to himself or his work or his designs. The younger generation passed by all his compositions no matter how unique they were, or perhaps because they were unique. All ears seem to have been deafened to his artistic goal, to the religious purpose of his music and its profundity, which came to be blamed for its artificiality, for its unnaturalness. Even his own sons lacked understanding and turned away from the music of the "old wig." Knowing that he had lost contact with his time through no shortcomings of his own, he hastened to prepare some of his works, not the great vocal compositions, but keyboard music, for publication—a tragic sight, indeed. This desperate attempt did not alter the situation, nor did it better his position. Completely forgotten, or completely unknown, before his death: such was the tragic fate which historical conditions, the rift between genius and environment, had shaped for Bach. It is a telling impression which we obtain from the historical constellation when we observe that young Haydn knew nothing of Bach and Mozart learned of him late by the whims of fortune.

Not the disfavor of a historical situation, not lack of recognition, but the temper of the artist led Mozart to arise as a tragic figure. It is true that the Viennese, said to be given to music by nature, found too much music in his composition; they thought it to be too heavy and never delightful. But such a misunderstanding, often the rule rather than the exception for great works of art, did not form the tragedy of Mozart; it accounts, perhaps, for the heartbreaking misery of his years in Vienna, but not for his tragedy. The tragic lay in his own demonic disposition, and none other knew it better than his father. The elder Mozart, unable to express himself adequately in accordance with the depth of his thought, always spoke in terms of the mediocre securities of life—and for that reason he was often misjudged—but he had, nonetheless, a notion, more emotional than rational, of what the nature of his son was all about. He lived in constant fear of the dangers which are bound to beset demonic natures, and his fears were justified. It is we who, seeing but the surface of a style to which Mozart clung throughout his life, quickly imagine that such stylish expressions as were his could not come from a troubled mind. In truth, style saved the artist, but not the man.

Given to excesses of exuberance and depression, he suffered all the ill effects of a melancholy temperament, in consequence of which he often gave a false coloring to the state of his affairs. Not that he ever misjudged music and musicians, but he misread the fortuities of his life. Misapprehensions reveal the tragic fissure of his demonic being. It is his demon who grants clairvoyance to his artistic mind, but blindness in the conduct of his life.

Divinely illumed he never erred in the realm of art; nor did he ever falter when an artistic crisis spun the web of complications. He held all matters artistic in masterly control; he overcame difficulties of artistic nature with ease more often than not; he approached artistic problems with that unswerving confidence which is unconscious of any obstacle on the way to the solutions. It might be that, because of the misfortunes and failures of the last years, he began perhaps to be more hesitant, but on the whole he owned the clairvoyant assuredness which comes from the demonic intelligence that, however bold and challenging the enterprise, he could not be mistaken in the chosen course.

Yet this propitious self-reliance, a blessing to the artist, had nonetheless its tragic consequence. For the artistic certainty which admits neither fear nor detrimental doubt led him astray, and wholly deceived by his infallible sense as an artist he cherished the costly illusion that the skills of art were also the skills of life. He fancied that his demonic assurance would be the trusted guide through the maze of life as it was for his artistic work. But the demon, however benevolent to Mozart the artist, decoyed Mozart the man into the snares of self-deception. Almost to the end he always trusted that he would master his life, that he would remove all difficulties with ease, that he would get the better of all vicissitudes. When in his later years misfortunes beset his path, he still did not see their gravity; he still misread their foreboding; he still uttered his blind hope and confidence that he would reverse calamity, although the truth of his situation permitted nothing but the darkest view. Like all demonic natures, Mozart strikes the beholder with the tragic terror. He discovered, in the end, his own tragedy and probably its reason. Abandoning his hopes and his assuredness, he surrendered to the tragic, fatal melancholy.

Perhaps, it is the Promethean tragedy which has been the most frequent, if unwelcome, caller among the visitors of artists. It even seems that all creative men hold the Promethean fate in the matrix of their being. Prometheus, the Contriver, is the benefactor of mankind. But for the benefaction Prometheus bestowed upon man by the gift of fire he suffered the most terrible punishment at the hand of Zeus. Pierced and chained to the rock by skillful Hephaestus, he—Prometheus Bound—was condemned to endure untold pains. Yet being the unerring seer of all things to come, he knew himself to be immortal, hence able to survive even the most cruel tortures, and he foresaw himself as Prometheus Unbound although his agonies would last through ages of eternity. And so, with all his prescience, he defied Zeus, his fate, and all afflictions.

Promethean tragedy embraces the artist fondly and with special favor. If the gift of fire set mankind upon the road of civilization, the artist who creates his beneficial work in testimony to human culture, is—like Prometheus—the benefactor of mankind. If Prometheus paid, for his charity, the penalty of suffering, the artist must—like a Prometheus—pay for his benevolence with the woes of creative contrivance. If Prometheus bade defiance to the wrath of God, the artist defies his fate because he—like Prometheus—foresees that his work outlasts his sufferance.

Although many a musician may be seen in the light of Promethean fate, it is Beethoven whom we behold as Prometheus revived. Driven by an ethical imperative, Beethoven contrived his art as a message to mankind. Others before him, Haydn expressly and Mozart implicitly, dedicated their music to the service of humanity; but Beethoven, in his quest for the shape of composition, persistently sought out the meaning of his work for the world at large, and from this meaning he gleaned the mission of his art.

When in his old age reflecting upon the purport of his music, Haydn owned that the knowledge of having his music contribute its modest share to the relief of man from the painful burden of the sorrows of life was the worthiest reward for all his efforts; in truth, the notion of such precious fruit had been the one and only—yet most powerful —incentive for him to keep going, as he said, even though the darkness of his own grief suggested a different advice. Beethoven, urged by his new energies, aspired to reach, beyond relief, the betterment of man, to bring about an ethical catharsis, the bliss which issues from Promethean benevolence. Early in his life, he became aware of the responsibility of art toward human ethics in the concealment of aesthetics.

When Beethoven was stricken by the affliction of deafness, he drew up the Heiligenstädter Testament, a document without parallel, addressed to mankind and written in defiance of a frightful fate. There he revealed for the first time, but not for the last, that despite all suffering inflicted upon him, suffering which for a moment set before him the alternative of suicide, he—like a Prometheus—would forever defy adversities and agonies. But the tragedy of life, the physical affliction, did not assuage the tragedy of art. Even the victory in the struggle with his destiny did not acquit the artist from creative suffering until his work had been completed.

The concepts of romanticism brought the tragedy of irreconcilable conflicts sharply to bear upon human existence. The old antagonism which carried many names in history but remained essentially the same discord between matter and mind, ideal and reality, infinite and finite, garnered an acutely subjective significance and deeply affected the newfangled sensibility of the romantics. "Man's unhappiness, as I construe"—and it is Carlyle who construes—"comes of his greatness; it is because there is an Infinite in him, which with all his cunning he cannot quite bury under the Finite." Thus, the romantic concedes, from the outset, defeat in his endeavors to draw into the rational form of the finite the infinite, the metaphysical, the irrational, that which cannot be grasped. None of his efforts can ever comprehend the whole; a remnant, large or small, will always be left out. And because of this the human mind never finds either peace or satisfaction.

When Victor Hugo in his *William Shakespeare*, brilliantly romantic in thought and poetical language, attempted to penetrate the mystery of genius, he took the attitude toward the infinite, the world of the unknown, to mark the point where man must make his choice. Those who, frightened by the searching view into the unknown, turn away from it, prefer the life of common men, a life of safety and a worthless peace. But those who do not fear the terrors of the search will be discoverers, the artists who make the unknown speak through bounded shapes. The price they have to pay is high: instead of safety, danger; instead of peace, disquietness; instead of comfort and content, perpetual unhappiness—the discord of divided souls.

Though life is forever marred by its incongruities, man has been given the boon of voiding the discrepancy, if only momentarily, in the work of art. For an instant his yearning for the lost paradise of harmony appears to reach its destination.

As profusely as romanticism furnished the creative mind with the conditions of a tragic existence, it also fomented the virus of a morbid disease; indeed, we often have been told of the romantic "maladie de langueur." The melancholy state of mind, both beneficial and malignant, can well be construed as the source rather than the effect of creative work; and there were romantics who anticipated the melancholy state in expectation of what was still to come and often did not come. Hence disillusions could not fail to play havoc among them. But melancholy always, and not only in the romantic age, held the potential of illness, and none other than Aristotle traced the symptoms when it took the turn to a disease. We, therefore, must not be too rash in observing symptoms of a "mal du siècle" when we approach romantic musicians, though we must be prepared to encounter tragic figures.

There have been attempts to rescue Schubert from the "maladie de langueur" by making him a "classic" composer. Yet it is rather the modern misconception of sentimentality, no doubt a "mal du siècle," which distorted Schubert more wantonly than any other musician. We do not right the wrongs of distortion simply by declaring him a "classic," whatever this might mean at the time when Schubert accomplished his work. And his accomplishment came to pass under the stress and strain which romantic antinomy had abundantly in store for him.

Letters, diaries, poems, autobiographies, all fondly favored by the romantics, add their precious evidence to the testimony of the art work. Revealing as such documents now are, they speed the probing of the musician's nature. They do so especially in the case of Schubert, who in speaking about music and his experience engaged the new romantic vocabulary with its own verbal rhythm and imagery. If his short story "The Dream" is really authentic, he paid a striking tribute to romantic views.

Where in his youth casual utterances speak from time to time of sadness and dismay, during the last five or six years of his short life melancholy released its hidden negative potential to develop a tragic crisis and to threaten the composer and his art. In a poem of 1823, called "My Prayer," he besought the coming of final deliverance, the end of what he said his life to be: a martyrdom. In a letter which he wrote the following year to a friend, the most personal document extant, the tensions of despair, still more stringent and more painful, appear to have pressed him to the very limit where one is faced with an ultimate decision. His perceptive mind prevented him, by the power of reason, from sweeping aside what he called the "fatal recognition of the miseries of reality," and his feeling, of greater intensity with him—as with all genius—than with ordinary man, could not cope with the rational dictum. Though he submerged in hopeless despondency, he conquered his despair; or rather, he succeeded in saving the energies of the artist to the last. But he rescued his creative energies only with complete resignation to the inevitable and irrevocable conflict with reality. He admitted his incapacity to pacify the conflict. Sacred art, as he said in another poem of 1824, the power of music, the musical art work should continue to soften human fate and blunt its thrusts. The "ethereal choirs" should never be disturbed, so he sings in his song "Auflösung," Disintegration (1824). Thus, the art work remained the only world of order in which he exerted himself to perform in opposition to the unmitigated disorders of life, not in Promethean defiance, but in expectance of death.

A medley, ever more entangled, of opponents contended in the divided soul of Robert Schumann, the soul of a romantic, to be sure, but one endowed with a nature too sensitive to parry the blows of the struggle. When Schumann gave the two discordant dispositions battling within himself the names of Florestan and Eusebius, he merely personified the abstract opponents of the romantic encounter. Yet his third personification, Master Raro, significantly an outsider, was to reconcile Florestan and Eusebius, to realize, by the reconciliation of the conflict, the synthesis of the artistic work. He knew that synthesis was not within the bounty of his nature, but without; hence he lived forever in fear that he might be denied the visitation of Master Raro.

As if to demonstrate the extreme consequence of romantic discordance, Fate added its scourge. It struck twice: once in 1844 and once in 1853, bringing to the fore all the frightful symptoms of Schumann's mental disease, schizophrenic psychosis.

Although there is every reason to believe that the disease was of hereditary nature, there is room for our conjecture that artistic tensions, fear of failure, tormenting doubts of the capacity to transfigure a fleeting vision into the constructive imagery of composition, nourished ill predisposition and hastened its fatal course. At times, we even waver, not knowing what is cause and what is symptom of his tragedy. For the discrepancy between vision and realization seems to lie at the root of the evil.

Seldom was there such a severe conflict between the clearest intelligence of the universally great and the awareness of limitations on the part of the composer. Such an awareness arose, of course, out of the doubts about his own faculties; and the doubts were as real as the deficiencies which made themselves felt whenever there was the question of sustaining the structure as a whole on the strength of the initial material.

Like all romantics Schumann thought and said that reason errs, but the heart does not. And since the initial inspiration was understood to spring from an incontestable source, the heart that never errs, Schumann's tragic calamity often derived from the primary misconception which, to his own misfortune, he never doubted, although the troubles which arose when he attempted to exploit the constructive productiveness of the material lay in the error of the beginning. Thus, he nearly reversed the meaning of Petrarch's word that reason speaks and feeling stings; with him it was reason that stung and feeling that spoke. The frightening vindications uttered at the time of mental derangement to justify his inspirations reverberate the heavy toll which insecurities have taken from the vital substance of the composer. Fateful nature provided a tragic disposition, incongruity between aspiration and ability, and the conflicts inherent in romanticism threw him into the benighted confusion with no escape from tragic catastrophe.

It rarely comes to pass that we can link to a single work the power of having turned the tides of history. This can be said of *Tristan and Isolde*. Although its impact was not felt immediately, in the end its thrust went deep down to the roots of the historical situation. It shook the foundations of style; it inculcated new conceits of aesthetics; above all, it procreated a new tragic constellation. Whether caught or not in the web of Wagner's lure, no composer could ignore the new drift of composition. Was the road Wagner laid open to be the only one that led to the music of the future as he triumphantly proclaimed? He had voiced contempt, if not Mephistophelean malice in speaking to musicians of his time. Go on, he told them, to compose symphonies, but rest assured that the enterprise will be a total waste; go on composing operas after the fashion of the past, but the effort will be, even at its best, no more than a flash in the pan. He did not mock in vain. For musicians of a different bent lost, indeed, their own security. New ambiguities, already abundant in the romantic age, accrued, and new artistic doubts, prone to sway from the salutary to the morbid, beclouded the musical scene. The loss of homogeneity in style and aesthetics, always the cause of precarious junctures, set free uncertainties to harrow the creative mind. It is again a period where tragic figures emerge from the complex of strained conditions, whether or not the individual artist because of his own nature lived with the strictures of a personal tragedy.

Brahms is such a figure, forced by Wagner through the narrows of tragic dilemma. What at first was for Brahms an unhibited attendance to the duties of a faithful heir—the heir to Beethoven, Schubert, Schumann—demanded at length, in consequence of Wagner, the heroic efforts of a struggle for survival. For Wagner impressed the ideal of Brahms with the aged traits of the past; he placed the distance of bygone times between himself and his younger contemporary who suddenly had to endure the painful effects of being thrown out of joint with his own epoch.

But in one respect, the aspirations of Brahms truly withered away under the shadow of Wagner. We often forget that at one time of his life Brahms, himself spellbound by the vogue of the Wagnerian music drama, made bold to seek his own approach to opera, one, we are sure, with which to remonstrate against the course of Wagner and to recapture, once again, the older schemes. Yet the upshot of all his protracted struggles was not an opera but—and this is not without significance—a song cycle of romances, Tieck's *Magelone*. Thus, fear arising as it did from a tragic constellation deadened the creative energy.

Even Verdi did not wholly escape the impact of Wagner, though the historical situation must not be fabricated after the fanciful novel of Werfel. Nevertheless, a portentous silence lasting a decade followed *Aida* and the Requiem. Determined to break off his artistic work, he parried all pleas for continued production with the defense that he had rendered his accounts in full, with no claims left unanswered; he had no more to say. Yet he looked with dismay upon Wagner, his followers, and the whole Wagnerian vogue, which he rebuked for having pushed musical politics into the realm of art, for having thus destroyed opera—that is, Italian opera. There lay the reason for his retiring into the solitude of deep skepticism and resignation. Despite the tragic mood of seeing his endeavor thwarted, he, in conclusion, summoned up his still unshattered strength to rise to the sublimation of his art, to *Falstaff* and *Otello*.

And *Pelléas et Mélisande* attained another triumph over the Wagnerian music drama as well as the traditional opera; but triumph came only out of tribulation. Claude Debussy—like Wagner, discontent, yet for different reasons, with schemes of composition sanctioned by the past; confused by the confounding complexity of music held in disorder by a fierce tendentiousness of schools; yet the born seeker with the vision of the new—proceeded along the thorny path of the modern artist. Nothing in his world of uncertainties, neither past, nor present, nor Wagner, eluded the test of the doubts of his unappeasable mind; and never did he trust inherited shelters, alluring as an easy safety, yet beguilingly fallacious. His fate of being born with the invested gifts of an innovator, but under the constellation of ill-protected values, rendered him a tragic figure, even though he succeeded in reaching the threshold of what we perceive as the music of our time.

And in our time, none other seems to have been stricken by a severer fate of tragedy than Arnold Schönberg. Let it hastily be added, however, that the conflicting components of our time throw the net of the tragic fiber over all of our intellectual endeavors. Surely, the historian has not always the right to lift, if he can, the mask of noble concealment from the face of a Bartók, or Anton Webern, or others unnamed. The tragedy of Schönberg, however, unfolded itself before the public eye, as it were, and he himself pronounced it to be the tenor of art both in the historical and aesthetical sense. He most emphatically insisted upon the necessity of his procedure, and having been deeply involved with Wagner, Richard Strauss, and Gustav Mahler, he thought himself to be faced with conclusions inevitably to be deduced from the historical constellation. Hence the conclusions he said he had been chosen to draw were not those of whim or fancy, but of necessity.

When late in his life he looked back to compositions not bound to the new structures, he tried to explain why he returned now and then to his old idiom. He revealed that he would have liked forever to cling to the characteristics of his early work "Verklärte Nacht," but fate, historical necessity, drove him away from what he liked to do into what he had to do. Precisely at this point the road of suffering began, where *melancholia generosa*, the beneficial melancholy of creation, turned into a *melancholia dolorosa* inflicting its harms with the sharp doubts about the artistic justification of the new. And the violence of public reactions to the new work added the pains of personal tragedy. Even the vilest of invective language was none too low to be flung year after year against the composer who, smarting with the stings of insult, had no weapon of defense. When Schönberg received the award of the American Academy of Arts and Sciences, he addressed to its president a letter, a document of his tragedy, which tells the story of a musician whom neither vicious attacks nor want of success could sway from the lonely path of his artistic conscience, conviction, and integrity.

Where do we stand today? Have present generations removed the tragic constellation under which the work of Schönberg took its rise? Past errors of injustice have been amended, and the late ascendancy of Schönberg over the artistic inspirations of a whole generation even seems to have indemnified Schönberg the artist for his calamities. But do such amendments truly lift the clouds which obscure the musical scene of today?

With a view to the whole range of the scene, we cannot fail to perceive a vast assembly of incongruities, the sum total of which does not, and cannot, flow together to an organic unity for the move in one direction. There is no such thing as a direction of our time, neither in life nor in art. All the components of the complex whole are fully charged with conflicting forces which pull the frame apart. But the contest between all of them, a spectacle for all of us to see, has its hidden counterpart in the individual, which is for none of us to examine. Surely, there are composers who are capable of reaching quick and easy decisions, often prompted by opportunism to come into the limelight of success. But success is no longer a criterion of value—perhaps it never was, at least not in modern times—and it does not tell the story of the struggles in the creative mind of today.

All the loose and irresponsible talk about the style or styles of music in our time reveals but one fundamental misapprehension: that "style" and "technique" are synonyms. Though we have mannerisms and techniques, we do not have style the strength of which appears to be determined by the uniformity of aesthetics, hence lastly by the resources of life. Our chance of attaining to a style of art is as little as the potential of our time ever to gain a style of life. And such a situation holds the tragic constellation ever present. But free from all the strictures of a pessimistic view, we believe that the history of artists is, and must be by its nature, the history of tragedy.

Acknowledgments

The quotation from Euripides, *The Bacchae*, on page 10 is from the translation by Arthur S. Way, Loeb Classical Library (Harvard University Press, Cambridge, Mass., 1950), by permission of the publisher. The quotation from Goethe on page 13 is from the translation by F. Melian Stawell and Nora Purtscher Wydenbruck, in *The Permanent Goethe*, ed. Thomas Mann (Henry Holt, New York, 1948), by permission of Dial Press. The quotation from Dionysius of Halicarnassus, *On Literary Composition*, is from the translation by W. Rhys Roberts (Macmillan and Company, London, 1910). All quotations from the works of Friedrich Nietzsche are from the translation by Oscar Levy (T. N. Foulis, Edinburgh and London, 1909–1913). Quotation from Aristotle, *Problemata*, is from the translation by E. S. Forster (Oxford University Press, London, 1927). All other translations are the author's.

Index

Index

Index

Index

Spectaculum mundi, 59, 61
Spontini, Gasparo, 79
Stile concertante, 62, 65–67, 74, 101
Stile recitativo, 54
Strauss, Richard, 127
Stravinsky, Igor: Orpheus, 46; Threni, 101

Tasso, Torquato, 70
Tassoni, Alessandro, 50
Tebaldeo, Antonio, 46; Orphei tragedia, 46
Templars, 87
Terence, 39
Tertullian, 41
Theognis, 8
Thomas, Dylan, 90
Tieck, Ludwig: Magelone, 125
Timotheus: Persians, 33
Tomkins, Thomas: "When David heard that Absalom was slain," 98
Traetta, Tommaso, 76; Antigona, 76; Sofoniska, 76
Tragédie lyrique, 17, 74–75
Tragicomedia, 47, 56, 66
Trissino, Giangiorgio, 48, 50; Sofoniska, 48
Trombones, 99–100
Tyche, 7–9

Valéry, Paul, 106
Vendramin, Paolo: Adone, 56
Verdi, Giuseppe, 93–94, 125–126; Forza del Destino, 79; Othello, 79, 82, 126; Libera me, 93–94; Messa da Requiem, 93, 125; Aida, 125; Falstaff, 126
Vettori, Piero, 54
Victoria, Tomás Luis de, 97
Vigny, Alfred de, 91
Villon, François, 103
Virgil, 70, 79
Vitry, Philippe de, 109

Wagner, Richard, 22, 26, 79–82, 124–126, 127; music drama, 21; Flying Dutchman, 79; Rienzi, 79; Tannhäuser, 79; art work of the future, 80; leitmotiv, 81; Parsifal, 81; Ring, 81; unending melody, 81; Tristan and Isolde, 81, 129
Wartenburg, Paul Graf York von, 27–30
Webern, Anton, 101
Werfel, Franz, 125

Zelter, Carl Friedrich, 15
Zeus, 1, 2, 10, 72, 117–118